DATE DUE

Liturgical Renewal in the Christian Churches

Liturgical Renewal
in the
Christian Churches

edited by
MICHAEL J. TAYLOR

HELICON
Baltimore—Dublin

Helicon Press, Inc.
1120 N. Calvert Street
Baltimore, Maryland 21202

Helicon Limited
20 Upr. Fitzwilliam Street
Dublin 2, Ireland

Library of Congress Catalog Card Number 67-13794

Printed in the United States of America

Preface

Christians have suffered a great division in their own sanctuary. Some have stressed the Eucharist with little emphasis on preaching the Word; others have carried on the prophetic mission of Christ almost as if there were no Sacrament. But many are coming to see that Christ is priest as well as prophet. His gospel is truly a message of salvation, an invitation to faith; but it is also a sacrament of faith and salvation. Both Word and Sacrament announce and communicate Christ's forgiveness and new life which only he can give who "died for our sins and rose again for our sanctification" (Rom 4:25). This risen Lord is eternally present to us in Word *and* Sacrament. And to be fully formed in Christ we must indeed listen and respond to his saving Word, but we must also actively share in his sacramental graces. This marks a change in the thinking of many Christians; what has brought it about?

The biblical renewal and early Church studies have helped to reshape the attitude of many. The New Testament, we now see, teaches us that Baptism can no longer be viewed as solely a Sacrament which institutionalizes believers; rather, it incorporates us into the Mystical Body of our Lord, makes us part of a new people of God, a public assembly formed to give true worship to the Father and committed service to the world in Christ's name. Certainly the new understanding of Scripture and Christian history confronts us dramatically with the reality of the Eucharist which was so central to the life of the early Church. Christians are

5

seriously re-examining what the New Testament understands by the Sacrament, what is meant by saying that the body and blood of Christ are really present in the Lord's Supper for our spiritual nourishment, and in what sense the Sacrament can also be called a sacrifice. The Churches are asking these questions again today, and this time Scripture is providing answers which unite more than divide believers.

And Christians have come to appreciate another common source for understanding the Sacrament, namely, the history of fifteen hundred years before the Reformation. By reviewing the belief of the Church before polemical positions were formed and hardened at the time of the Reformation, Christians are re-discovering lost insights and are finding that they can modify statements made in controversy, not necessarily by changing them radically, but by integrating them with a fuller historical view of salvation. Patiently and thoroughly researching into the meaning of the Eucharist at the exegetical, historical and theological levels, Christians are meeting the mystery anew, probing further into its depths, expressing it in contemporary terms, always of course respecting the traditional beliefs of the Churches. Protestants, Orthodox and Catholics are doing this, and the effort has brought us remarkably close together in our understanding and appreciation of the Eucharist (I believe a reading of these essays will show this and illustrate to Catholics that liturgical revival among Protestants and Orthodox is a matter of real substance and thus a great source for ecumenical hope).[1] Certainly the liturgical renewal operative in every segment of Christian life by restoring a meaningful sacramental life has worked a great renewal in the hearts of believers.

And coincidentally, the liturgical and biblical renewals

1. The Catholic reader is advised that these essays were not originally written for a Catholic audience and therefore occasionally some doctrinal distinguishing is needed. Significantly, however, such distinguishing seldom is necessary.

have quickened within us a real concern for Christian unity. The early Christians were substantially one in faith and ritual; to persevere in division is a scandal the Churches find increasingly painful to countenance. They desire to show forth their present oneness and to work and pray for Christ's grace to overcome the remaining obstacles to unity. This is why ecumenists in the World Council of Churches are anxious to realize more comprehensive intercommunion among their members. The Lord's Supper is seen as the great Sacrament of unity, the way that Christ himself wants us to manifest and effect the unity of Christians with himself and with each other: "Because the bread is one, we the many, who partake of the one bread form one body" (1 Cor 10:17). And even though many frustrations have resulted from attempts to realize intercommunion, still the efforts to accomplish it have intensified the search for an understanding of the Sacrament of Christ's presence which all Christians can accept in good faith.[2]

Protestants are re-discovering in his eucharistic Presence a personal encounter with Christ; but the Sacrament has other meanings and purposes (meanings also accepted by Catholics, but until recently largely neglected). It is, for example, especially a source for awakening a sense of Christian community and social responsibility. Sharing the Lord's Supper together, they regard the sacred meal, like all family meals, as a means of effecting a more solid fellowship with each other; and sharing in the common bread of Christ they are made aware of their common dignity, equality and

2. The reader is referred to Max Thurian's full treatment of *The Eucharistic Memorial,* and the Faith and Order report, "Worship and the Oneness of Christ's Church" (Montreal, 1963). This consensus reflects solid biblical and liturgical scholarship and shows how highly regarded sacramental worship is among Churches of the World Council. A Catholic exploratory statement of the problem can also be found by Michael Redfern, "Freedom of Worship: Intercommunion," in *Christians and World Freedom* (Helicon, 1966).

brotherhood. And moreover we can see in Protestant use of the Sacrament efforts to relate participation in the banquet to the ongoing mission of the Church to the world.[3] The Eucharist is surely nourishment and source for fellowship among Christians, but also a commission to and sustenance for the sometimes demanding task of bringing Christ's Spirit and grace to men.

And Protestants and Catholics alike are gaining from Eastern Christians a new awareness of the eschatological dimension of the Sacrament. Our earthly banquet is seen as a preparation for the eternal. The glorious Christ is present in mystery, bestowing his Spirit who becomes in us the pledge or guarantee of the full possession of God in eternity. In a world fragmented by anxiety, tragedy, war, hatred, and injustice, the meal of the Eucharist stands as Christ's unshakable promise that eternal peace, order and joy await us hereafter.

And of course there is renewed appreciation of the sacrificial nature of the Eucharist. Many Protestants have reconsidered the Reformation position which looked upon Christ's Sacrifice as something wholly of the past, which satisfied divine justice in full and ended forever the age of altar, sacrifice and priesthood. Many now see in the Lord's Supper something more than a grateful commemoration of a sacrifice. Some are speaking of Christ's eucharistic offering. As Christians offer themselves, their souls, bodies, praises and prayers, it can be said in a manner that Christ with whom Christians are united by mystical union in the Sacrament offers his Sacrifice with us and we offer it with him.[4] To say

3. See, for example, the essays of E. S. Brown, G. Webber, and D. Webster.

4. A typical expression of this "new position" is found in a statement of the bishops at the 1958 Lambeth Conference, commended to the careful "study of all the sections of the Anglican Communion": "Christ's sacrificial work on the Cross was *for* us; he died as our Redeemer. He

that we are offered, as Protestants maintain, and that Christ is offered, as Catholics insist, need involve no contradiction, since what is offered is both Christ and Christians, who are united by virtue of the mystical union that exists between the head and members of the Church.

Thus the whole idea of eucharistic sacrifice is being re-examined. Should the "new thinking" continue along present lines it can only have the good effect of bringing Catholics and Protestants much closer in belief on the extremely controversial issue of the Eucharist as Sacrifice. Since the Sacrifice of the Altar was at the center of the religious conflict of the sixteenth century, and remains one of the central obstacles to Christian reunion in the twentieth, the import of the "new thinking" for Christian unity should be obvious.

And as Christians study more deeply the meaning of the Lord's Supper, they discover in its celebration unitive purposes never before fully appreciated. Godfrey Diekmann has said that in the "whole vast contemporary movement of ecu-

---

who once died and is now alive for ever more is also *in* us; he dwells in our hearts by faith. And in virtue of this union, we are now identified with him both in his death and passion, and in his resurrection, life and glory. There is but one Body, of which he is the Head and we are the members; and we are made one with each other because we are one in him.

"In our baptism we were united with him by the likeness of his death (Rom 6:5) and in the Eucharist we abide in him as we eat his Body and drink his Blood (John 6:56). So we come to the Father in and through Jesus our great High Priest. We have nothing to offer that we have not first received, but we offer our praise and thanksgiving for Christ's sacrifice for us and so present it again, and ourselves in him, before the Father. We are partakers of the sacrifice of Christ (1 Cor 10:16), and this is shown forth by our sacrifice of praise to God continually through Christ (Heb 13:15), and by our life of service and suffering for his sake in the world (Phil 3:9-10). We ourselves, incorporate in the mystical body of Christ, are the sacrifice we offer, Christ with us offers us in himself to God." (Lambeth Conference *Report*, part 2, p. 84). See also the essays of M. Thurian and R. Greenacre.

menism, the most significant single factor is the Eucharist—celebrated and received in fact or in desire. Through the Eucharist, God has been and is laying grace foundations of unity."[5] Common reception of the Sacrament has always been accepted as a manifestation of the unity of the Church; now more and more Christians are beginning to see the Sacrament as instrumental in effecting that unity. Called to enter the Kingdom of Salvation, Christians are made members of their Lord through faith and Baptism and are sustained and nourished in the unity of his Mystical Body through participation in his Sacramental Body. When early Christians met at the Lord's Table and received his Body and Blood they knew that they were being formed into more than a social group for religious ends; they believed that they were being united with the real Christ and in that union were being bound together in a new, redemptive fellowship with each other.

> Does not the chalice of blessings which we bless bring us into union with Christ through his blood, and does not the bread which we break bring us into union with Christ through his body? Because the bread is one, we the many, who partake of the one bread, form one body (1 Cor 10:16-17).

Koinonia in the Body and Blood of Christ effected the *koinonia* of his Mystical Body. As Max Thurian has said so well, Communion unites the faithful indissolubly with each other:

> If the Church makes the Eucharist, the Eucharist makes the Church. The Eucharist unifies and joins together the members of the body of Christ: those who have been baptized are joined together in unity and can but seek the deepening extension and

5. G. Diekmann, O.S.B., "The Eucharist Makes the People of God," *Jesus Christ Reforms His Church* (Washington, D. C.: The Liturgical Conference, 1966), p. 105.

fulfillment of charity, which it supports and extends . . . In the life of a local community the Eucharist is the place where the Church is built up and deepened in charity. That Church which celebrates the Eucharist frequently beholds Christ through the Eucharist, developing his charity, his unity, and making his word and his life effective in the world.[6]

And Thurian's words but reflect the ancient eucharistic traditions of the Church. It was Cyril of Alexandria who said of the Sacrament:

> To merge us in unity with God and among ourselves, although we have each a distinct personality, the only Son devised a wonderful means: through one only body, his own, he sanctifies his faithful in mystic communion, making them one body with him and among themselves. Within Christ no division can arise. All united to the single Christ through his own body, all receiving him, the one and indivisible, into our own bodies, we are the members of this one body and he is thus for us the bond of unity.[7]

And so the Sacrament has meant and still means for many not only the mystery of the Sacrifice and Real Presence, but the Sacrament wherein Christ makes and unifies his Church. In the Eucharist Christians are discovering what they are and are receiving from Christ the grace to become more of what they are, his very Body.

Thus in the understanding of the Eucharist many Catholics, Orthodox and Protestants seem to be converging toward a remarkably common faith. This is certainly not to say that total or near-total agreement in sacramental theology is at hand, for we have only begun to inquire into the exact meaning of contemporary statements on the Eucharist. Only continued and honest discussions will show if our views are

6. Max Thurian, *The Eucharistic Memorial,* Pt. 2 (London: Lutterworth Press, 1960-61), pp. 120-24.

7. *In Joannem,* 11, 11 P. G., lxxiv, 560.

as close as they seem. From the Protestant side, for example, there has not yet been extensive investigation into the role of the minister in worship, nor have Catholics generally reviewed their position in light of the teachings of Vatican II[8]; this is an extremely important aspect of sacramental worship and in our present understanding we seem far apart. Also, the Catholic liturgist grows a little depressed at even now reading occasional Protestant descriptions of the Mass as a "repetition of Calvary" as though it were somehow a denial of the universal efficacy of Christ's once-for-all Sacrifice, or as though it were a Sacrifice in some way separate from or opposed to Calvary. This was a false reading at the time of the Reformation[9] and is a false interpretation now. Still, we have come a long way in understanding each other and these essays should increase understanding and provide observations and insights that can be helpful to all of us in our efforts to renew the liturgical life of the Church. The time for serious inter-faith conversations on the Eucharist is long overdue; it is hoped that these essays might act as partial preface to such conversations. We are in a position to help and inform one another. Having become in many ways interdependent in the development of sacramental and liturgical theology, it seems most desirable that we unite in a common effort to search for an ever fuller understanding of the eucharistic mystery.

Obviously we have much more biblical, historical and liturgical soul-searching to do before we stand united in Christian fundamentals, but now we can approach the task with the common conviction that the Eucharist is not inci-

8. A recent exception: See, F. J. van Beeck, S.J., "Towards an Ecumenical Understanding of the Sacraments," *Journal of Ecumenical Studies,* III, 1 (Winter, 1966), 57-112.

9. F. Clark, S.J., *Eucharistic Sacrifice and the Reformation* (Westminster, Md., Newman Press, 1960).

dental to the search. Nor is it in any way in opposition to the Word; both are of the utmost importance to Christian life and worship, and indeed are Christ's two great means of making us one.

MICHAEL J. TAYLOR, S.J.

Seattle University
Seattle, Washington

Acknowledgments

Grateful acknowledgment is made to the following authors, editors and publishers for permission to use material under their copyright:

To Weibe Vos, Editor of *Studia Liturgica* (The International Ecumenical Quarterly for Liturgical Research and Renewal, Mathenesserlaan 301 c, Rotterdam, Holland) for permission to reprint the following articles published in *Studia Liturgica:* "The Liturgical Movement and Christian Unity," by A. M. Allchin (Vol. 1, March, 1962); "Worship and the Cross and Resurrection of Christ," by Harald Riesenfeld (Vol. 2, June, 1963); "Worship and the Ascension of Christ," by Boris Bobrinskoy (Vol. 2, June, 1963); and "The Worship of the Church and Modern Man," by Edgar S. Brown, Jr. (Vol. 2, March, 1963); to Belknap Press (Harvard University) for permission to reprint "Word and Sacrament in Protestant Worship," by Cyril C. Richardson from *Ecumenical Dialogue at Harvard: The Roman Catholic-Protestant Colloquium,* edited by S. H. Miller and G. E. Wright (Cambridge, Massachusetts, 1964); to James Clarke & Co. for permission to reprint "Meaning of Holy Communion," by Nicolas Zernov from *Orthodox Encounter* (London, 1965); to Lutterworth Press and John Knox Press for permission to reprint sections of *Eucharistic Memorial* by Max Thurian (London, England, and Richmond, Virginia, 1960-61); to George W. Webber for permission to publish "Worship in East Harlem"; to the Faith Press for permission to reprint "The Passover of Christians,"

15

by Roger Greenacre from the *Sacrament of Easter* (London, 1965); to William B. Eerdmans Publishing Company and SCM Press, Ltd. for permission to reprint "Come, Creator Spirit! For the Renewal of Worship and Witness," by Thomas F. Torrance from *Theology in Reconstruction* (Grand Rapids, Michigan, and London, England, 1965); to Seabury Press for permission to reprint "Liturgy or Cult: Source or Resource?" by Massey H. Shepherd, Jr. from *Liturgy and Education* (New York, 1965); to the Society for the Propagation of Christian Knowledge and Douglas Webster for permission to reprint "The Mission of the People of God" from *The Parish Communion Today* (London, 1962). The editor wishes also to express his special gratitude to Canon Don H. Copeland, D.D., Director of the World Center for Liturgical Studies at Boca Raton, Florida, who provided the facilities of the Center's library to help research a number of these essays.

Contents

17

*In our frequent converse with Christian people
we often recall the words of that great religious
thinker, Bossuet: "There is no fulfillment in
religious work or in Christian life except in participation in the Eucharist." Our whole mission
to the world should flow from participation in
the Sacred Mystery . . . it is from the altar, the
holy table, that we must view, judge and make
use of the things of this world. Even the most
difficult questions that confront men must find
in the Eucharist the point of departure for a
just solution.*

Lateran Basilica, 1958

The Liturgical Movement
and Christian Unity

ARTHUR M. ALLCHIN

There are two movements within Christendom that on the surface are not apparently connected. There is the movement for liturgical renewal, and there is the movement which has Christian unity as its main interest and goal. In the liturgical movement the stress falls on worship; it is in the first place an effort to give Christian forms of worship a new life and meaning. It is, at first sight perhaps, something of an inner Christian concern; but it is in fact concerned with much more than forms of worship, because it involves a re-thinking of the nature of the church and its relation to the world. It asks Christians to reconsider the content of their faith. The movement has started, in different forms, at many different points in Christendom, and its only obvious connection with the ecumenical movement is the remarkable way in which it has drawn separated Christians together through common interests and activities.

There is however a common feature in these two movements. Both have arisen spontaneously; and while both have expressed themselves in various new organizations, neither has been controlled centrally. Until a few years ago, the ecumenical movement had seemed to center entirely on the World Council of Churches, which brings together for study, consultation, and practical work the great majority of

Protestants and Eastern Orthodox Christians. But since the election of Pope John XXIII, it has become clear that the Roman Catholic Church, too, is vitally concerned; so that the unobtrusive but valuable work of a number of Roman Catholic scholars and thinkers in this field has received open approval and a new impetus. At the General Assembly of the World Council of Churches at New Delhi in November 1961, there was a much fuller Orthodox representation than before, and for the first time Rome was represented by official observers.

EXTERNAL AND INTERNAL PRESSURES

It might well be asked, since Christians have for centuries been prepared to live more or less contentedly in mutual isolation, whether this new-found solidarity is merely the product of the pressures of twentieth-century life. Is it, for instance, that the churches fear the challenge of communism or of modern secularism, and come together in order that they may not fall separately, by political suppression or a process of attrition? Or does it represent a more genuine growing together of the separated Christian bodies, corresponding to some inner development within them?

It would be absurd, I think, to deny that the pressure of outside events has had something to do with the development of the ecumenical movement. Without it, and without all the modern possibilities of travel and exchange, large-scale Christian collaboration during the past fifty years would have been impossible. But I believe it would be equally wrong to suggest that outside pressures alone have brought this movement into being. The World Council of Churches has always firmly resisted the temptation to "make a common front against communism." It has always embraced Christians from both sides of the Iron Curtain, and has always tried to maintain a sharp distinction between the Christian attitude towards man and society, and the practical "materialism" current in the West.

Indeed it is doubtful whether the movement towards unity could have gotten this far if it had been only a response to external pressures. And certainly if it were only externally motivated then whatever unity might result could never be more than adventitious and superficial. From within Christendom, at any rate, it does appear that there is a real convergence of traditions, a real meeting and mutual enrichment, a genuine learning from one another in such a way as to overcome the old parochialism and willful misunderstanding. It is in this *inner* development that the liturgical movement has a crucial function. In various though often unspectacular ways, it contributes to the steady convergence of practices and ideas. On the Roman Catholic side—if I may quote Father Charles Davis—it has involved reasserting "the central place of the Bible in the church, and the practical bearing of this for teaching and piety, and the living power of the word as preached."[1] It has also brought about a new appreciation of the active role of the laity in the worship and work of the church.

On the Protestant side there have been complementary developments: a perception that to be properly understood the Bible must be set in its primary context, that is, within the life and worship of the church. Protestants, too, have tried to show how the laity are actively and not merely passively members of the church. They have needed to do this; for though the sixteenth-century Reformers did a lot to make services more intelligible, they did not give the laity much of an active part in them. And whereas from the Roman Catholic side, the centrality of the Bible and the preaching of the word have been reasserted, from the Protestant side, there is a new readiness to acknowledge the Lord's Supper,

1. Charles Davis, *Liturgy and Doctrine* (New York, 1961).

the Communion or Eucharist, as the culminating point of Christian worship. It is more frequently and more solemnly celebrated in the family gathering of the local church. The sacrament is no longer divorced from the proclamation of the word.

THE PRESENT EXTENT OF AGREEMENT

We have reached a position in which—it is fair to say—there is a measure of agreement among Christian scholars of most diverse backgrounds as to what the central act of Christian worship should be: a eucharistic celebration, in which both word and sacrament have their part, in which the whole congregation shares as actively as possible, and in which the predominant note is one of Easter joy and of thanksgiving, for each Sunday is a renewal of the day of resurrection. In all churches the weight of convention holds people back from fully realizing this vision; they may not everywhere be conscious of a "liturgical movement" and may sometimes think only in terms of copying the traditions of another more "liturgical" church. This does not take away from the importance of agreement among the more reflective members. That is unexpected—in the light of history, perhaps even astonishing.

The "converging" process that I have been writing about is strikingly exemplified in church building. It becomes increasingly difficult to distinguish Roman Catholic Church buildings from Protestant ones. The Roman Catholic bishop of Aberdeen, for instance, has recently been criticized for making his cathedral as bare as a Presbyterian kirk, by removing all superfluous decoration, and concentrating attention on the plain altar-table, around which God's people meet. Within Anglicanism, where differences in the ornaments and decorations of the church were for long infallible pointers to "high" and "low" churchmanship, the new movement has created a salutary confusion. For on the "high" side there is a desire to get rid of redundant decoration, and on the "low," a new readiness to take seriously the symbolic nature of the building and of what is done within it.

For the Protestant, generally speaking, this new emphasis on the Eucharist and the sacramental in Christian faith and worship involves a deep change of attitude towards space and time; for these can no longer be treated as irrelevant to the worship of God. Questions of symbolism take on fresh importance when it is recognized that the central act of Christian worship involves the use of material things and symbolic actions. The common meal of the Eucharist is held to hallow the whole range of human activities. Time is "sanctified," and through a renewed understanding of the church's seasons, acquires a new importance as a means by which the rhythms of personal life may be related to those of earth and heaven. It offers a way by which we may be rescued from that predicament which D. H. Lawrence describes when he speaks of "a poor, blind, disconnected people with nothing but politics and bank-holidays to satisfy the eternal human need of living in ritual adjustment to the cosmos and its revolutions."

NOT ONLY A MATTER OF SERVICES

Of course, if the liturgical movement were just a matter of rearranging church services and church interiors, or of perceiving a new significance in certain traditional Christian patterns of worship, one might still be inclined to regard it as something of relatively minor importance. But in fact the effects, starting from the center of the church's life, spread out into the whole of its activity in the world. The very word "layman" acquires fuller meaning; and the sense of the unity which ought to exist between the church's inner and outer life grows greater.

I hope I have shown that by the nature of its central concern, the renewal of the eucharistic meeting of the church, the act by which the Christian community is constituted, the liturgical movement has an immediate link with the question of Christian unity. For it is coming to be more and more widely recognized that it is in the Lord's Supper that the center of unity must be found; in the act, that is to say, through which the Christian people renew their unity with Christ and with one another.

All this brings us only to the outskirts of the subject. What has been described so far might still be regarded as a sort of "setting to partners," in which Roman Catholics find themselves extolling simplicity and the preaching of the word, and Protestants aspiring to more symbolism or to the monastic tradition.

But the matter goes much deeper. It reaches down to the roots of doctrinal disagreement within Christendom, to those intractable issues of dogma which underlie all our more peripheral disagreements. It takes us down to that area of given common ground which is the basis of all work and hope for unity among Christians, and it begins to show us ways by which separated Christians may discover themselves talking a common language, and if not agreeing with one another at all points, at least being able to carry on an intelligent and intelligible conversation.

THE HEART OF THE MATTER

The doctrinal core of the liturgical movement, as I see it, is the doctrine of God. And here I quote from a prophetic but little-known Anglican writer of the nineteenth century, R. M. Benson: "I am very glad," he writes in a letter to a friend, "of what you say about the doctrine of the Blessed Trinity. It does seem to me to be the root evil of the present day, the want of pure theology. People are full of disputes about sacraments, eternal punishment, inspiration and the like; and yet the people who know a great deal about these controversies know next to nothing about the Holy Trinity. But this is the Creed. The others are only corollaries of the Creed, and are helpful or hurtful just in proportion as they are made subservient to this fundamental doctrine—valueless, even when rightly held, if their connection with the eternal relationships of the Blessed Trinity is not recognized. Our doctrine, teaching, experience of the Church, must be, so to speak, in a comatose state, unless there be an active, experimental, living knowledge of the Name of the Holy Trinity, which is the living power wherewith the Church is bound together by the Holy Ghost."[2]

In this passage Benson expresses his conviction about the nature of the Christian faith, a conviction which he shared with his more famous contemporary, F. D. Maurice. He points to the heart of Christian belief, to the revelation of God's name and nature in the Son and Holy Spirit, in St. Irenaeus' phrase, the two hands of the Father. It is here that one finds the common ground for all Christian thinking and experience; and all other Christian doctrines are to be seen in relation to it.

Here, too, is one of the basic interests of the liturgical movement, in its desire to put this doctrine back into the center of the church's life. Hence the power of the movement as a reconciling, unifying force. For while there remain many unresolved differences between Catholicism and Protestantism, by tracing their origin back to the common belief in one God in Trinity, and placing them in that context, one begins to see openings for mutual comprehension, which were certainly not apparent before.

You may wonder how it is that this basic doctrine, which has never been repudiated in the vast majority of Christian

2. R. M. Benson, *Further Letters* (1920), p. 220.

communions, has yet somehow faded from the general consciousness of Christian people in the West. In his recent book, *Liturgy and Doctrine,* Father Davis has faced the problem from the Roman Catholic side. He has indicated the way in which, through the liturgical movement, it is hoped to restore this doctrine of the divine name and nature as a living reality for the people of the church. The point is significant for the question of Christian unity because this failure to hold together the whole structure of Christian life and doctrine around its central point is a feature common to both sides in the West. And—what is still more significant— it is *not* a characteristic of Eastern Orthodoxy. Whatever the shortcomings of Eastern Christendom may be, the doctrine of the Trinity has remained there "the unshakeable foundation of all religious thought, of all piety, of all spiritual life, of all experience."[3]

So the scope of the liturgical movement may be seen from the fact that it has not only brought Catholics and Protestants nearer to one another, but both into living contact with Eastern Christendom—a part of the Christian world where the liturgy has never been cut off from the common life and worship of the people, and has never lost its character of a glorification of "the Kingdom of the Father, of the Son and of the Holy Ghost."

WHAT HAPPENED AT THE REFORMATION?

What finally does all this imply for our attitude towards the sixteenth-century Reformation in Europe—a cataclysm, an upheaval rather than a movement—and one which, so far from being a unifying force, tended to divide and disrupt Western Christendom? Here we have to face one of the most radical changes of historical perspective which our twentieth-

3. Vladimir Lossky, *The Mystical Theology of the Eastern Church* (London, 1957), p. 65.

century reformation sets before us. The more one studies the development of Western Christendom, the more one is struck by the way in which the twelfth century seems to be the period from which many of our present problems spring. It is no coincidence that it was exactly at this time that the split between East and West was becoming final, and the West was setting out on that one-sided development which led to the brief glory of the middle ages, and the long subsequent disruption. Seen in this perspective the whole upheaval of the sixteenth-century Reformation is not the grand climacteric of Christian history—nor even the *first* reformation or disruption—but merely one episode in that subsequent development; an episode which proved particularly inconclusive because of the inadequate assumptions which both parties inherited from the Western middle ages. One can see now how radical our twentieth-century reformation really is; it has enabled us to see how much both Catholics and Protestants in the earlier reformations were united, paradoxically enough, by the things which divided them. It has also given us a chance to breathe the fresher air of patristic Christianity.

It is not at all easy to pin down the exact nature of the break in the Christian consciousness which took place back in the eleventh and twelfth centuries. The difference about the "filioque clause," the addition to the Creed of the statement that the Holy Spirit proceeds from the Son as well as from the Father, may only be a symptom of some deeper malady. But it is surely not the irrelevant dispute over words that many have thought it to be. For it is precisely around the question of the way in which the Holy Spirit works in the individual, in the church and in the world, that many of the later disagreements cluster. The centralization of spiritual, juridical power and pastoral authority in the hands of the pope—the vicar of Christ (but is not that the Spirit's

role in church?)—is one sign of this. Another is the altera-
tion in the relations of the church to the temporal power,
with the fateful outcome which that had for the place of the
laity. From then on the history of Western Christendom
became increasingly the history of a struggle between individual and institution. That struggle had been largely transcended before, because the church had been seen not primarily as an institution but as the communion of the Holy
Spirit.

THE RECONCILING POWER OF THE LITURGY

I would claim no kind of finality for this interpretation. But
it follows a line which appeals at the present time to scholars
of quite different background and church allegiance, and
promises to be extremely fruitful. What the liturgical movement is doing in our own day is not so much *creating* a new
unity among Christians, as bringing to light that common
ground which they already share. And its unifying effect is
not only or even mainly in bringing together separate Christian denominations. Rather it is bringing together separated
elements within the one Christian tradition, complementary
aspects long thought of as being antithetical. Thought and
devotion, worship and action, can no longer be kept apart.
Bible and Eucharist come together and illuminate each
other. The unity of clergy and laity within the body of the
church is envisaged in a new way. The new emphasis on the
activity of the laity reaffirms the bond between all human
activity and the mind and life of God. In all this the liturgical movement is gathering up the riches of Christian tradition, not in a spirit of antiquarian revivalism, but driven by
the sense of participation in the life of the risen Christ.

If one asks: then is the liturgical movement backward
looking?, "yes" is certainly part of the answer; but its interest in Christian origins is always joined with concern for the

situation of the church here and now. In the new reformation, we go back, not to the past, but to the heart of the Christian mystery, to the divine nature as it is expressed in the Christian revelation.

Is it then justifiable to speak of a modern reformation? So far as one can now see, the church must at this time make ready to face the growing challenge of secularism, in its more or less ideological forms, and the first meeting with the other great religions. For these formidable tasks the prerequisite is not merely to be united but to be seen to be so. One can only wonder whether the current developments in Christendom—the liturgical movement, the ecumenical movement—exciting and creative though they are, will be enough to make the needed reformation; or whether still greater pressures from outside must first bring us to a more radical repentance.

Word and Sacrament
in Protestant Worship

CYRIL C. RICHARDSON

Owing to the wide diversity of Protestantism it is not possible
to give as clear and comprehensive a survey of its worship
as is possible in the case of Roman Catholicism. While the
Latin rite is, of course, not the only one in Roman Catholicism, and there are a number of Uniat rites in different
languages, nonetheless, there is a basic uniformity which
characterizes the vast majority of Roman Catholic liturgical
observances. With the churches of the Reformation it is different. Yet there are fundamental leading themes characteristic of all Protestant services and these we shall survey. We
must, however, always bear in mind that the wide range of
Protestant services is such that different emphases have
tended to characterize the various denominations, and
throughout Protestant history there has been no fundamental
pattern universally observed.

Before treating the basic concerns of Protestant worship,
it is well for us to bear in mind the large dependence of
Reformation liturgy upon the forms of worship in the later
middle ages. Originally Protestant services were revisions
of the Roman Mass and of the medieval vernacular service
of Prone, which was inserted in the Mass before or after the
sermon. Furthermore, a type of devotional piety centered in
subjective meditations characterized the Lay Folk's Mass

Books which were widely used in the late middle ages. Not a little of the Protestant attitude toward the Holy Communion ultimately derives from these layman's handbooks.

It is thus important to note that in the realm of worship the Reformation represented a continuity with the medieval past as well as a revolution. In the general structure of the service, in the quality of devotion, in the emphasis on the passion of Christ in the celebration of the Lord's Supper, and finally in the continuing idea that the congregation should basically remain passive, there is a clear connection with the Mass of the later middle ages. On the other hand, the Reformation stands as a revolution in introducing a fundamental emphasis upon the word of God, upon the need for corporate worship and for greater intelligibility as well as simplicity. It is noteworthy that many of the features in the schema of the Second Vatican Council have a direct parallel in the concerns of the Reformers. In consequence, it is likely that the Catholic services will become more like Protestant ones just as, under the impetus of the current liturgical revival, Protestant services are recovering something of their Catholic past and becoming more like Roman ones. This presages well for an eventual unity of the spirit among Christians insofar as they appreciate the many diverse facets of worship and grow closer together in their common concern for the life in Christ.

BASIC CONCERNS OF PROTESTANT WORSHIP

Let us now look at some of the basic concerns which have dominated Protestant worship throughout its history. While these concerns have been given varying emphases among the differing denominations, nonetheless they may be said to be characteristics in general of Protestant liturgy.

The first one is this: That the *Word* may prevail. By the Word of God the Reformers meant first and foremost God's disclosure of himself in Jesus Christ. This revelation of God in his freedom is given in the words of Scripture as well as in the sacramental acts of the church. Fundamentally, however, it means the declaration of God's forgiveness and the condescension of the divine love in our redemption. It was this aspect particularly which Luther stressed in his liturgies where the warmth of piety centering in the grateful recognition of the divine love is dominant. For Calvin, on the other hand, the word means primarily the declaration of the *gloria Dei*. This is, of course, not without the note of the divine love, but it gives peculiar prominence to God's transcendence. There is a word of Calvin that very well expresses the whole character of his services: "We are born first of all for God and not for ourselves."

Because the word is something that is spoken directly to man's understanding in God's self-disclosure, the importance of the sermon and the reading of the Scripture in the vernacular are primary concerns of the Reformers. Luther, for instance, in his *Formula Missae,* writes, "But the important thing is this, that everything be done so that the word prevails and does not become a clamor or a whine and rattled off mechanically as it has been heretofore." Or again, "Where God's word is not preached, it is better that one neither sing nor read or even come together." Hence, it has been characteristic of Lutheran worship that even at sacramental services a sermon is regarded as essential. Unless man is given the opportunity of hearing the word of God and of intelligently grasping the character of the divine revelation, worship descends to superstition. Calvin equally is concerned with this importance of the presentation of God's revelation by sermon and Scripture. He writes in the *Institutes,* "The principal object of the sacrament, therefore, is not to present us the body of Christ simply . . . we never rightly and advantageously feed on Christ except as cruci-

fied and when we have a lively apprehension of the efficacy
of his death." It is this "lively apprehension" that is the
fundamental point of worship. Sacramental forms can so
easily fall into superstition, the intoning of prayers in a
foreign tongue can become so unintelligible, that the full
significance of participating in the disclosure of the divine
glory and love in Jesus Christ becomes obscured.

It is for this reason that the reading of Scripture itself
becomes sacramental. In the place of the snippets from the
epistles and gospels, which the English reformers used to
refer to as "pisteling and gospeling," the Reformation
stressed the need for much longer passages of Scripture and
full and adequate expositions of them in the sermon. The
sermon characteristically took on the quality of instruction,
and indeed the use of the scholar's gown became indicative
of the relation of the minister to the congregation. In some
ways the educational and instructional character of worship
was overemphasized and its more prophetic meaning, along
with its more mystical elements, tended to be obscured.
However, the large emphasis given to Scripture and its exposition was basically an attempt to speak directly to the worshiper about the divine condescension in Jesus Christ.

As a result of the emphasis upon the word, there was a
consequent decline of sacramental worship. While all the
reformers except Zwingli wished that the celebration of the
Lord's Supper should be the normal form of Sunday worship, nonetheless the tendency for there to be only a preaching service quickly asserted itself. There were many reasons
for this. There were, on the one hand, political reasons, as in
Geneva, where the town councils refused Calvin's insistence
upon weekly celebrations of the Lord's Supper because they
feared riots and opposition of the people who might imagine
the Roman Mass was being restored. Another reason had to
do with the infrequency of communicating in the later mid-

dle ages. The rule which had been laid down by the Fourth Lateran Council of communicating once a year at Easter was widely followed and attendance at Mass was generally not for the purpose of receiving the elements. Consequently, when the Reformers stressed the corporate character of worship and insisted that the Lord's Supper should only be celebrated when all communicated, celebrations became infrequent, since the people were disinclined to break their medieval habit. The service of the sacrament could not be celebrated with no one or only a handful to participate. Thus, the Protestant service really became a *missa sicca,* in which the service of the word, derived from the synagogue, stood alone without reaching its consummation in the sacrament.

Yet a deeper reason for the decline of the sacrament must be observed in the theological understanding of the Lord's Supper which dominated the thinking of the Reformers. They tended to view the Holy Communion as a reduplication of the word. Thus, if the word had already been preached and the Scripture read and expounded, what was done in the Lord's Supper was merely a repetition of the same thing. It expressed in more tangible and visible form what had already been accomplished in words. We shall revert again to this point, but it is perhaps the deepest reason why the celebration of the Holy Communion became monthly or quarterly as a consequence of the Reformation.

The second fundamental concern of Protestant worship was that superstition should be made impossible. There should be no "hocus-pocus," which actual phrase is a corruption of the Latin words of consecration, *"hoc est corpus meum."* The white walls and the streaming daylight from the large windows of New England churches are symbolic of this desire to have everything clear and in the open without any possibility of reverting to magical tendencies. A number of features of Protestant worship come directly from this concern. Intelligibility was stressed above the sense of mystery. Everything was to be done aloud and spoken in the vernacular, so that there could be no misunderstanding. The feeling which had developed from the fourth century, that the consecration prayer should be said in a subdued voice because of the character of the liturgical mystery, was something quite alien to the Reformation spirit. Then, again, simplicity was a dominant concern. Cranmer's objections to what he calls "dumb ceremonies" indicate a typical spirit of the reformer. Elaborate worship was now superseded by the most simple forms, as having less danger in them and as being more directly intelligible to the congregation.

Finally, the sense of corporate worship was emphasized over against priestcraft. For example, in the revisions of the Roman Mass which the Reformers undertook, a number of the ancient prayers in which the priest addressed God in the first person singular were converted into the first person plural, in order to indicate that the minister is the leader of the congregation rather than one who mediates between the congregation and God. Furthermore, the emphasis upon psalm singing in the simple Genevan tunes gave point to this feeling for corporate worship, just as the requirement that the Lord's Supper should be celebrated only when the people were willing to communicate, equally emphasized the communal character of worship. All these concerns were directed against any identification of the religious symbol with the reality to which it points. Superstition, which did to some measure characterize the late middle ages, was to be offset by a type of worship in which the congregation could participate with understanding and without the dangers of magic. This, of course, posed very serious problems for Protestant worship, in that there was always a tendency for the symbols to be divorced from the realities to which they pointed, and the rational forms to be so emphasized that the sense of mystery in worship was overcome.

A third dominant concern of Protestant worship was that the free Spirit of God should be given opportunity. This was particularly developed in the left-wing Reformation among Independents, Congregationalists, and Baptists. Here the emphasis fell first upon extemporaneous prayer. The immediate, direct experience of conversation with God was to supersede written and traditional forms of prayer. Even the Lord's Prayer was regarded as inadequate for public worship because it could be rattled off mechanically and did not have that immediate and spontaneous freshness which the more left-wing reformers felt to be the note of true worship. John Cotton, for instance, could write in 1642, "Nor will it stand well with the holy gesture of prayer, which is to lift up our eyes to heaven, if we cast our eyes down upon a book." This is a typical Puritan attitude to the Anglican *Book of Common Prayer*. Barrow could ask, "May such old, written, rotten stuff be called prayer? May reading be said to be praying?" Or, again, John Owen could write, "All liturgies are false worship (and not the English only), used to defeat Christ's promises of gifts and God's Spirit." There was a consequent opposition to written sermons as well as written prayers. Worship was to be conducted in such a way that one would be open to the immediate and direct influence of God's Spirit and not bound by traditional forms.

This implied giving emphasis to intimacy in worship. In the small congregation of devoted believers, fellowship with God was looked upon from the point of view of a direct and immediate relation in which the worshiper gave personal utterance to that which the Spirit of God evoked in his heart. Not only the minister but the layman prayed aloud, prophesied, and exhorted. Certain of the extreme forms of such worship, in speaking with tongues, religious dancing, and so forth, were developed in the more radical of these groups.

Finally, it must be observed that a certain tension between form and freedom has been characteristic of Protestant worship precisely because of this desire to stress the free Spirit of God. Only in the Anglican communion has there been an attempt to enforce uniformity. In general, classical Protestantism has tried to relate form to freedom by providing model services and model prayers, but allowing the minister a good deal of latitude in their use and composition. Calvin himself was not averse to a set form of worship. He even urged its usefulness, contending that it was "to help the unskillfulness and simplicity of some . . . that the consent of the churches with one another may appear . . . that the capricious giddiness and levity of such as effect innovations may be prevented." Yet the forms he provided for Geneva were models rather than forms which had to be followed in detail by the minister. His attitude, as that of Luther, was the same which had characterized the ancient church. Hippolytus had provided his liturgy in the *Apostolic Tradition* as a guide to Zephyrinus, the bishop of Rome, whom Hippolytus as a learned scholar seems to have felt was in need of some guidance. In the general Protestant scene today some measure of form and freedom is to be observed in practically all denominations, and indeed the 11 o'clock Sunday service is rather similar in the large Protestant bodies.

The final basic concern of Protestant worship has been the revival of the liturgy of the ancient church. It was the desire of the Reformers to recover the way of worship in the New Testament and the early period. This was the Reformation counterpart of the Renaissance concern to return to the sources. The motto was *ad fontes*. Hence Calvin could subtitle one of his liturgies, *"Selon la Coustume de l'Eglise ancienne."* It is for this reason that the Reformers felt that word and sacrament belonged together; and indeed Calvin himself regarded their separation as "a vicious custom," and annual communion as a veritable "invention of the devil." We have already indicated some reasons why the sacrament tended to decline in importance, but it must be stated that the early Reformers, while they did not have the scholarly resources we have today for understanding New Testament and early church worship, nonetheless were vitally concerned that there should be a return to the original forms of worship in the Christian church.

The modes of worship that characterize the Protestant denominations today are beginning to betray an increasing uniformity. There is a general Sunday morning service in the Presbyterian, Methodist, Lutheran, and Congregationalist traditions which, while there are differences in detail, nonetheless has assumed a basic pattern. It opens with a choral procession and with a sentence from Scripture, which is followed by a confession of sins and absolution. Then there is a responsive reading from the Psalter followed by hymnody or a chant. After this there comes the morning lesson and then the pastoral prayer, which may be a single long prayer or divided into shorter collects. The service tends to reach its climax in the sermon, which is followed or preceded by an anthem, the collection of alms, and a hymn. The service concludes with a benediction and a recessional.

This structure in essence is, of course, the first part of the Mass. There have been many changes but the main outline of intercessory prayer, psalmody, and sermon goes back to the synagogue service that the early Christians inherited from Judaism.

While a good deal of variety is introduced into the service of the word, in the celebration of the Lord's Supper the specific forms of the different denominations tend to be more closely observed. These differ in the various churches, but there are now emerging "ecumenical" liturgies that attempt to recover a good deal of the Catholic past while still preserving fundamental Protestant points of view. Perhaps the most notable of the ecumenical liturgies has been the Anglican, for Cranmer attempted to weave together many diverse sources in his book. In the Holy Communion, the basic structure and a good deal of the material comes directly from the Sarum Use, but this has been modified both by Protestant concerns and also by materials derived from Lutheran and other liturgies. In the middle of the nineteenth century in this country the Mercersburg liturgies appeared. They were a notable contribution since the leaders of that movement of the Reformed Church in America, namely Nevin and Schaff, had a concern for recovering the Catholic heritage. One might also note the liturgy of the United Church of Canada: the uniting Methodists, Presbyterians, and Congregationalists made use of their diverse liturgical heritages, weaving them together in a common service. The more recent revision of Lutheran liturgies both in Sweden and the United States has recovered the traditional pattern of the consecration prayer in the place of the *verba* of the typical Lutheran liturgy. In the Congregational Church in the United States the *Book of Worship for Free Churches* shows how very much the liturgical revival has affected that communion. A similar revision of the *Westminster Directory* has now been undertaken and will doubtless issue in an equal concern for recovering the Catholic elements of the past. Perhaps the most notable ecumenical liturgy of the modern day is that of the Church of South India, which has united Catholic and Protestant elements with rare skill and success. Equally interesting, though less influential, is the Taizé liturgy of the French Reformed community, which is dedicated to church unity and of which Roger Schutz and Max Thurian are the distinguished leaders.

The characteristics of these ecumenical liturgies are, first, the attempt to recover traditional structures; secondly, the preference for biblical language in the central prayers where there have been the keenest theological divisions; and, finally, the introduction of responses that heighten the congregation's participation in public prayer. The responses inserted in the consecration prayer of the Church of South India are particularly significant in this connection.

There are a number of other factors that make for ecumenical liturgy among Protestants. One of these is hymnody. Increasingly Protestant churches sing hymns from every period of the church's development, and indeed one might say that in the realm of hymnody there is the most notable ecumenical spirit. Again, the recovery of the church year among Protestant groups who formally disavowed it has been important. Nowadays not only Easter and Christmas, but Epiphany, Lent, Advent, and a number of holy days such as All Saints are observed. Then, too, the introduction of silence into worship has been a sign of learning from other denominations. This has not grown extensively, but the impact of Quakerism on Protestant worship is not to be underestimated. Finally, the architecture of churches, in which there has appeared the "divided chancel" with the altar in the center and the pulpit at the side, has indicated a desire among Protestants to return to a type of architecture which did not give undue prominence to the pulpit and which followed the norm developed in the early basilica and the Gothic church. In all these ways there has been a movement toward a recovery of the Catholic heritage without compromising the basic concerns of the Reformation.

MEANINGS AND ANTITHESES

The point at which there has been the greatest division in the tradition of Protestantism concerns the understanding of the Lord's Supper. Here the issue of the meaning of religious symbols has been acutely debated and no resolution of the matter is yet in sight. However, in a number of ways to which we shall return later, some advance appears to be possible today; and even a measure of reconciliation with basic patterns of Catholic thought is not out of the question.

The early Protestants took sharpest exception to the Roman Catholic doctrine of transubstantiation. Here a number of issues were involved. In the first place, most of the Protestants approached the doctrine of the Lord's Supper from the point of view of a nominalist philosophy, in the structure of which transubstantiation was either meaningless or superstitious. What was affirmed by all parties was that after the consecration the bread remains bread and there is no conversion of its inner substance into the body of Christ. Furthermore, the majority of Protestants laid emphasis upon the element of subjectivity in sacramental religion. They felt that the Roman Catholic doctrine unduly stressed the objectivity of the sacrament; and while in many ways they attempted to preserve the sense of objectivity, they wished to correlate it more deeply than Roman Catholic theology had, with the subjective dispositions of the recipients. Basically one can say that the general viewpoint from which the Protestant doctrine was worked out was that which had been characteristic of sacramentals in the Roman tradition. The doctrine of *ex opere operato* was denied, and in its place emphasis was put on *ex opere operantis*. That is to say, the significance of the sacraments did not lie only in the objective act of God and of the priest, but rather in the action of God that was apprehended by the act of faith. One other point is of some importance, namely, that Baptism was regarded as a pattern to which the doctrine of the Lord's Supper should conform. In Catholic theology a sharp distinction between these two sacraments was made, and the *res sacramenti* was regarded as present in the consecrated elements in a way that it was not in the rite of Baptism. It is this approach to the Lord's Supper from the doctrine of Baptism that gives point to the Protestant concern for *ex opere operantis*.

The three basic doctrines that were devised were those of Zwingli, Luther, and Calvin. We may briefly characterize them in this way. Zwingli regarded the elements of the Lord's Supper as picturing the past event for faith. In him there is a fundamental split between spirit and nature, so that the things of nature do not participate in the divine but rather give a symbolic expression to that which is grasped by faith alone. The significant action of the Lord's Supper falls in the realm of spirit, mind, and consciousness. Faith, to be sure, is regarded as a gift of God. Zwingli even refers to it as a *res*. Nonetheless, the transaction of the Lord's Supper is one in which faith is fortified by God and the outward elements are merely picturesque ways of reminding the believer of God's act in Jesus Christ. The fundamental emphasis, furthermore, falls upon the deep gratitude of the believer for what is done in Christ, and therefore the leading theme of the Supper is *eucharistia* (thanksgiving) for a benefit already received. Zwingli does not, of course, deny the presence of Christ in the Supper. Rather does he say that he is present by his divine nature, and that all talk about participating in the body of Christ is metaphorical for the reception by faith of the benefits brought by the passion. The body of Christ, in any literal sense, is inaccessible because in heaven, and irrelevant to the action of the Supper. Religion has to do with mind and spirit, not with matter. This clear-cut distinction fitted the type of mathematical thinking that was developing; and the general position has been furthered by the spirit of our technological age in which the autonomy of nature, separated from the world of spirit, has been given undue weight.

In Luther a quite different doctrine emerges, and one which is marked by some originality. For Luther, the action of the Lord's Supper is much more integrally connected with the world of nature, so that the divine is mediated through material forms. Luther emphatically denies transubstantiation partly because he is a nominalist, but also because he regards transubstantiation as an act of *man* which seeks to win God's favor, and hence is indicative of work-righteousness. Rather does Luther see the Supper as the gift of *God* for man who can do nothing on his own to win salvation. It is not possible for the Christian minister to convert the substance of the bread into that of the body of Christ by means of the consecration. Rather is something done by God for *us* in the consecration. What this is, is the manifestation of the hidden ground of existence. By means of the *verba* of consecration, the body of Christ, which is ubiquitous and everywhere, is made accessible so that it can be grasped by faith. This is what Luther means by the *esse repletive,* a category that he adds to the modes of Christ's presence, which had been worked out by Occam. For Luther the body of Christ is the hidden mystery in, with, and under all things. The body of Christ cannot be looked upon as an object seated on a golden throne in a transcendent heaven. He vehemently attacks Zwingli's view as involving a childish view of God. The "body of Christ" is an expression in Luther for the basic religious reality underlying all creation. Thus, when the *verba* are said, that which is present in "every loaf of bread on the table, in every leaf on the tree," is made manifest and accessible. The ordinary loaf on the table contains the body of Christ no less than the loaf on the altar. The point, however, is that in the loaf on the ordinary table the body of Christ is hidden and inaccessible, whereas on the altar it is revealed and made available. God appoints a word in terms of which the mystery of his being behind all existence is *greifbar*—made accessible to the believer. While in Lutheran dogmatics the full implications of Luther's own position were not always accepted, nonetheless the sharp distinction between Lutherans and other Protestants has been on this question of the objective presence of Christ in the sacramental elements.

Calvin attempted to steer a middle course between that of Zwingli and Luther. He worked out with great clarity what had been begun by Melanchthon and by Bucer. This view can be expressed in terms of the complementarity of physical action and spirit. While the bread is not regarded as in any way changed by virtue of the consecration, or as participating in the divine, nonetheless, the physical action is viewed as having attached to it the promise of God in such a way that when the Lord's Supper is celebrated a spiritual transaction between God and the believer takes place. The locus of this transaction is the realm of spirit, mind, and consciousness. Calvin tends to explain it in two ways. Either by the virtue of God's Spirit, the body of Christ in heaven is brought to the believer so that he "participates in some measure in Christ's immortality," or, on the other hand, the spirit of man is raised by God to the heavenly realm, there to partake of the body of Christ. The objectivity of the action is greatly stressed. It lies in God's promise that when the physical actions are performed a corresponding but not integrally related action between God and man's spirit occurs. In the *Consensus Tiguriensis* (The Zurich Consensus) the Calvinist and Zwinglian positions were brought close together. This has, by and large, been the doctrine of the Reformed Church.

On the question of the sacrifice in the Lord's Supper, the Protestant position gave the emphasis to three things. In the first place (as is made clear in a recent book by Aulén[1]) the

1. G. Aulén, *Eucharist and Sacrifice* (Philadelphia: Muhlenberg Press, 1958).

once-for-all-ness of the cross is given the great stress. In no way can the Lord's Supper repeat it, nor can the action of the Supper participate in the cross as if the latter were a transcendent and timeless reality. Rather is the emphasis placed upon the uniqueness and the *Einmaligkeit* of the passion. Thus, the Catholic doctrine in connection with the sacrifice of the Mass is excluded. In its place the Protestant liturgy expresses the themes of the sacrifice of ourselves, our souls and bodies, and also the sacrifice of praise and thanksgiving. Many texts from the early church which deal with the latter type of sacrifice are quoted; and insofar as the early Fathers attacked the literal sacrifices of pagan and Jewish religion, there is a close connection between the Protestant mind and that of the early church. However, it must be observed that the full implications of the early doctrine were not grasped by the Reformers.

From these basic ways of looking at the Lord's Supper, a fundamental antithesis between the Protestant and the Catholic viewpoint arose. There was a contrast for one thing between table and altar. For the Protestant the table of the Lord's Supper was the table around which the faithful gathered to receive that which God promised, but in no way to participate in an actual sacrifice. Then again there was a contrast of prophet and priest. Protestants stressed the prophetic element of the word, whereby the declaration of God's forgivenesses was made, over against the action of the priest in converting the substance of the bread into that of the body of Christ. Finally, we may observe the contrast between the surplice and gown, on the one hand, which were the vestments of Protestants, and the chasuble and alb on the other, which were the traditional eucharistic vestments. The surplice was a medieval development for the choir offices. The gown was either the scholar's gown, as Luther had used it to preach in, or else the gown of the upper bourgeoisie, which Zwingli had adopted in the Zurich services and which was similarly taken over in Geneva. These vestments symbolized the service of the word as a choir office, or the educational significance of the exposition of Scripture. The chasuble and alb, on the other hand, while they had their origins in the normal wear of the upper classes in the later Roman Empire, had taken on a sacrificial significance. This occurred in the ninth century when a Judaizing movement overtook the Church in the early middle ages. When dress had sufficiently changed for the alb and chasuble to seem somewhat esoteric, they were given the meanings attaching to the priestly vestments in Leviticus. In consequence they came to signalize the garb of the sacrificing priest.

NEW EMPHASES TO OVERCOME THE ANTITHESES

It is clear from what we have already said that the basic antitheses of the sixteenth century are still with us. Reconciliation between Catholic and Protestant positions appears impossible if we continue to think along the lines which led to the sixteenth-century separation. It presages well, however, for some possible ecumenical theology which will gather together both Catholic and Protestant insights, that the stark divisions of the Reformation are coming to be viewed rather as overemphases on both sides than as truly expressive of the meaning of the Lord's Supper and other sacramental forms. It is patent, for instance, that the concepts of table and altar cannot be separated. If, on the one hand, the significance of the Lord's Supper leads to the Communion as the corporate act of the fellowship of Christ, then, on the other hand, sacrificial ideas cannot be excluded from the Lord's Supper. It is a sacramental act whose significance lies in its relation to the total sacrifice of Christ, and in consequence the altar is not a concept which can be excluded as if it were irreconcilable with the idea of table. In actual fact, table and altar in their Hebrew as well as in their Greek equivalents are words which interchange. An altar is a place on which an offering is made, and this very place is itself a table, for every offering culminates in a communal feast. Similarly, the contrast between prophet and priest cannot be held to be one of mutual exclusion. The word is not something which cancels the priestly act of the sacrament, but rather word and sacrament belong together in a mutual fulfillment.

Perhaps the most fundamental point at which to begin some reconsideration by means of which these antitheses can be overcome is the notion of worship itself. We are all familiar with the commonplace that worship in its linguistic origin is connected with the word "worth," and worship gives expression to that which man prizes most highly. This, however, while it may be satisfactory for a theology based on the idea of value (as Ritschlianism, for instance), is not fully satisfactory. The underlying notion in worship is that of *being,* the word "worth" itself coming from the Anglo-Saxon *weorthan,* which means "to be." Worship is the act in which man recovers his being in relation to God. He overcomes the split between himself and his ultimate ground. All worship, therefore, must be looked upon not merely as the expression of what man values, but rather as the means by which man discovers the true meaning of his existence and realizes the basic nature and the destiny for which God intended him. In this light, we have a much larger concept in terms of which we can look at different aspects of the act of worship.

A second helpful approach is that of realizing that the concept of sacrifice cannot be limited to that of death. In this regard all Western theology, whether it is Roman Catholic or Protestant, has tended to lay undue weight on the notion of sacrifice in connection with the passion of Christ. Sacrifice actually is a much broader term. It means to "make holy"—*sacer* and *facere*. The process of making holy, or recovering one's "wholeness" in relation to God, involves much more than the concept of death. At least four fundamental notions are implied, and all of these should find expression both in the actual liturgy as well as in the understanding of the Lord's Supper. These four moments of the sacrificial act are offering, dying, rising, and finally participating in the eschatological banquet. The significance of the Lord's Supper is that it presents the total sacrifice of Christ in such a way that the believer can participate in it and re-enact it in his own being. There is first offering, that is to say, the abandonment of the self to God. There is then dying, the actual experience whereby the ego-centered nature is crucified. But that leads to resurrection. We rise with Christ, and this finds its fulfillment in the communal banquet that gives expression to the End. This banquet is both a present realization of the heavenly sphere and also an anticipation of the final fulfillment. Here both future eschatology and realized eschatology are united. In this larger concept of sacrifice, then, we see worship as the total act in which there is presented the whole work of Christ in such a way that we are able to live through it ourselves and participate in that which he has accomplished in terms of human nature. This further leads us to a consideration of the way in which the sacrificial action of the service so presents Christ that his perpetual relation to the Father is made manifest and made accessible. It is necessary at this point to go beyond the idea of the one-for-allness of the cross, to appreciate its significance as the historic expression of the eternal reality of the divine nature. It is because the divine nature is love that the sacrifice of Christ is an eternal act and is thus able to be made present in worship here and now.

A third important consideration in our rethinking of sacramental forms is the notion of participation. In the act of worship we "re-call," "re-present" that which has already been done but whose significance lies beyond the historical moment in which it was done. There is an actualization of Christ in and among us, and not merely a remembering of what was done in the first century A.D. Here it is important that due weight be given both to the objective and to the subjective aspects of sacramental worship. It lacks reality if the subjective experience of faith is played down. But it lacks power if there is an insufficient appreciation of the way in which the act of Christ is objectively present. The outward forms are not merely reminders of something that was once done, but are themselves the vehicles through which the eternal significance of what was done is made available. Hence there may be a way of speaking about the sacrifice of the Mass in such a manner that elements of superstition can be eradicated, and all talk about repeating the cross (which certainly is not genuine Catholic talk) can be avoided.

The mystery theology of Odo Casel is perhaps of some help in this connection. It may indeed be said that he derived his material too much from Hellenistic religions and not sufficiently from the biblical notion of *anamnesis*. It would, perhaps, be better to take such a celebration as that of the Passover to bring out fully the significance of biblical "remembering." In the biblical notion, the community is able to relive the events of the past and make them genuinely their own, because of the corporate personality of the group. The Jew in celebrating the Passover does not think of the crossing of the Red Sea as something which happened to people long ago. Rather is he bidden to think of *himself* as one who was rescued from Egypt, because he is a participator in the heritage of the people of Israel. In the same way, the church understands that the crucifixion occurred not only in the first century, but occurs in some sense in connection with us here and now. We are the inheritors of a tradition. We are the heirs of the early disciples. And thus in the act of worship there is made present, in a way in which we can grasp it and be grasped by it, the eternal significance of what was once done in Palestine. These events are present events as well as past events, and the whole significance of the act of worship is to make present the past in such a way that we are able to relive it in ourselves and thus recover our true being and destiny. It is along lines such as these that perhaps we shall be able to overcome the false antitheses that were posed in the sixteenth century, and achieve some vital reconciliation between Catholic and Protestant understandings.

The Meaning of the Holy Communion

NICOLAS ZERNOV

For the Orthodox the Holy Eucharist stands in the center of
the Church's life. It is the God-given source of strength,
purity and unity. From this point of view it is only to be
expected that the forces of distintegration should concentrate their fiercest attacks upon this stronghold of the new
covenant. The most bitter controversies have been waged
over this sacrament, and nowhere else is the shame of divisions more clearly revealed than in the unwillingness of
Christians to meet around the Lord's table.

One of the consequences of this broken fellowship is the
impoverishment of the meaning of the Eucharist, each
denomination having underlined one side of its purpose. The
separated members of the church being deprived of the fullness of the sacramental life are thus prevented from being
led into the shelter of the one undivided fold.

The recovery of a more balanced eucharistic practice and
teaching is one of the most urgent tasks confronting those
Christians who seek a return of visible unity. The Eastern
apprehension of the Eucharist is for this reason essential and
complementary to the Western tradition. The Eucharist, as
seen by the Orthodox, offers not only promise and means of
salvation, but is also a cure for the disruption of fellowship
among the redeemed people.

Jesus Christ built his church on the eucharistic foundation. The incarnate Lord did not formulate any creed as the

53

means of communion between God and man; he elaborated no ecclesiastical system to protect his followers against heresy and schism; he even refrained from giving them any precise rules for moral conduct. But on the night when he was betrayed, he gathered his disciples round a table, broke bread and blessed the cup, commanding them to do this in remembrance of him until he came again. The Eucharist is the gift the God-man left with his followers, promising them remission of their sins, defense against the powers of evil, and revealing to them the task which they are called to fulfill on earth under the guidance of the Holy Spirit.

The purpose and character of the Eucharist are in complete harmony with God's treatment of men as shown by the Old and New Testaments. God seeks the free and responsible cooperation of his creatures, and he chooses therefore the most natural means of securing man's assistance in his plans. Thus, the daily cleansing by washing is raised to the mystery of spiritual purification and rebirth in the sacrament of baptism. The incorporation of a new member in the Christian community is performed by the laying on of hands and anointing, the traditional gestures of blessing and welcome. The breaking of bread is exalted to communion between God and man. It offers to its participants strength to overcome their self-centeredness, lifts them beyond the boundaries of nation, class and family, and opens their eyes to the vision of the full meaning of the incarnation.

To those who are ready to learn from it, every meal imparts a deeper understanding of men's nature and of his true relation to the rest of creation. The physiological process of eating and drinking transforms inanimate matter into a source of free and creative activity. A prayer is offered, a poem recited, a symphony played, a picture painted, and scientific truth is discovered, because men and women, by eating and drinking, enable matter to surpass the limitations of time and space and to be restored to harmony with the spiritual order.

Eating and drinking also reveal the interdependence of human, animal and plant life. Man needs food, and this reminds him that although his fulfillment is in the realm of the divine, his roots go down into the same material substance found in the remotest constellations and in the smallest physical particles. He is the apex of a pyramid to which all earthly organisms belong, but man differs from animals and plants in having to use his inventive mind to secure his food. His study of the seasons, the cultivation of plants, the breeding of animals, and his determination to control nature all arise from his dependence on food for survival. Food also brings home to him that his fate is not only in his own hands, but is controlled by the same power which provides the fruits of the earth and sends the wind and the rain. Such are the great lessons to be learned from every meal; but their full significance can only be seen in the light of the Holy Eucharist.

The Eucharist contains all those elements of renewal and instruction offered to man through his daily food, but it has in addition some unique properties essential to his spiritual growth. The first is what Nicholas Cabasilas, the great Eastern theologian and mystic of the fourteenth century, calls the "human" character of the food offered at the Eucharist.[1] Its participants are invited to receive the bread and wine which are the product of human toil, the fruit of the combined efforts of many men and women. At each Eucharist, not only the celebrant and the communicants have their honored place, but also all those who have sown the seed, gathered the harvest, ground the corn, baked the bread and brought it to the church; all those who have tended the vines,

1. Nicholas Cabasilas, *A commentary on The Divine Liturgy* (London, 1960.)

crushed the grapes and turned them into wine. The whole process of human industry is therefore sanctified through the Holy Writ. When Jesus Christ ordered his disciples to break sacramental bread and drink sacred wine, he blessed all human labor and elevated the work of man's hands and the inventiveness of his brain to the highest level of making it the acceptable offering of the creatures to the Creator.

The second distinct element of the Eucharist is its universality; all humanity is invited to it, of whatever race, nation, culture or class. An ordinary meal is the traditional expression of trust and friendship between those who take part in it; but it can also be used as an instrument of separation; it can be a manifestation of family, class or tribal allegiance excluding all outsiders. The Eucharist alone has no such limitations; it is a feast prepared by the Savior for all men, and the only condition of admission is the faith in the incarnation, confirmed through Baptism and the readiness to forgive those who offend us.

The third element of the Eucharist is its significance as a covenant. It has a special mystical sense attached to it, for it contains a commemoration of the old covenant and a re-enactment and bringing to fulfillment of the new covenant. God calls men to work with him, and at the Eucharist Christians respond to this appeal by remembering God's mighty deeds in the past, and the acts of faith performed by their forefathers. The communicants accept their moral obligations towards their fellow men and the rest of creation, sure in their trust in the God who brought them out of Egypt, the land of bondage, and delivered them from sin by the incarnation of his Son. The Eucharist foreshadows the coming of the messianic kingdom and invites the willing participation in it of all the faithful. It reminds Christians that they are the elect, since they have been given the task of making the kingdom of God shine so brightly in their midst that the world can submit freely to the lordship of the son of man.

Fourthly, the Eucharist signifies a sharing in the sacrificial death of Christ, and is the blessed fruit of his glorious resurrection. The elements used for this sacred rite reveal the hidden link between life and death, passion and resurrection. The grain must fall to the ground in order to spring to new life; the grape must be crushed before it can be made into wine. The Eucharist is inseparably bound up with the agony in the garden, with Christ's betrayal, crucifixion and death upon the cross. It makes clear that there is no easy road to the kingdom, that nothing short of complete victory over self can bring men into the fellowship of the Holy Spirit. But formidable and terrifying as the forces of evil may be, they are incapable of holding down the Light under cover of darkness; they can distort, but they cannot annihilate the image of God in man; they can seduce and poison the minds and undermine the will-power of Christians, but it is beyond their power to close the door to repentance or to nullify divine forgiveness.

The Eucharist proclaims that the Christian belief in a God of love is not wishful thinking, it reveals the truth of divine compassion, which makes certain the final victory of good over evil. God himself shared with men all their sufferings and degradations in order to give them a tangible proof of his love for his creation, a love which does not destroy the freedom and independence of those whom he would have as his willing co-workers in the building up of his kingdom.

Fifthly, each Eucharist is a cosmic drama in which the whole of mankind plays its appointed part. It unites all human beings with the body and blood of Christ, creating an indissoluble oneness among all believers and establishing a bond between the living and the faithful departed, and especially with the one who gave birth to Jesus Christ, the virgin mother of God. Although subject to rivalries and passions, those who partake of the Eucharist differ from other men because, by the grace of God, they are the instruments by which the Holy Spirit enters into the body of mankind and through it sanctifies the cosmos.

Finally the Eucharist is the meeting place between Jesus Christ and the believer, personal, intimate, unique. It makes the Christian a new creature by elevating him into the divine presence, and in that transcendental unity his individuality is eternally affirmed and reconciled with the infinite variety of the whole creation. In the Eucharist Christians possess the power that can secure their victory over all the temptations of the intellect and of the flesh; they are restored by it to unity and concord in the fullness of communion with the holy and life-giving Trinity.

Thus the Eucharist is the foundation of the Christian community. A church centered in the sacraments ceases to be merely an ecclesiastical institution or a convenient meeting place for people interested in religion. It becomes a divine leaven, which slowly but surely transforms the earth by deifying men and by sanctifying matter through the mystery of the Lord's Supper. The Eucharist creates a sense of partnership and confidence between men and nature, and drives away the fear of the material world which haunts men outside the Christian community and makes most non-Christian civilizations so barren in the field of applied science. Man's understanding of the universe and his ability to control it are the fruits of the eucharistic experience. The conquest of space and time, the struggle against disease, oblivion and death, the whole growth of modern civilization, is rooted in eucharistic worship. In spite of the misuse of power, in spite of narrow-mindedness and quarrels, Christians possess in this sacrament a force which has helped them to change the face of the earth, to make mankind its true master and which, moreover, contains still greater potentialities for those who are ready to be reconciled with one another and lovingly obey the will of their Creator.

Such an interpretation of the nature of the Eucharist does not deny its more commonly accepted significance as the means of salvation and of reconciliation; but it considerably enlarges the sphere of sacramental action and sees man as no longer an exile on earth from his true home in heaven, but as a spokesman for the whole creation, responsible for the redemption of all other beings. Man's salvation depends therefore not on his moral behavior alone, but on the dedication of all his creative gifts to the work of transforming the universe into the messianic kingdom.

Worship in East Harlem

GEORGE W. WEBBER

INTRODUCTION: EXPOSURE AND FREEDOM

The frustrations and failures of Protestantism as it faces
modern urban culture in America have given an inner city
ministry like the East Harlem Protestant Parish a quite
unique opportunity to serve the whole church. Here, in a
congested, racially heterogeneous, low-income neighborhood, the various denominational churches are brought into
head-on collision with the facts of modern urban life in
their sharpest and harshest form. The emerging world of
mass man, with all its forms of depersonalization, is exposed,
and we see how individual dignity and responsible human
life are being destroyed. At the same time, the inadequacy
of current patterns of church life are also exposed. Largely
carried over from a rural culture, they are quite unable to
meet the challenge of the city. We like to speak in East
Harlem of the "Gift of the City," for in the very act of confronting us in the city with the failure of our old patterns,
God is reminding us that we must look again, as did our
Reformation ancestors, for his patterns for the new day in
which we live.

Because the East Harlem Protestant Parish is interdenomi-
national, with mission support from seven major denominations (American Baptist, Presbyterian, Congregational
Christian, Methodist, Reformed, Evangelical and Reformed,
and Evangelical United Brethren), it has been granted a

quite unique freedom to seek for the "new wineskins" for the church's life, unfettered by ecclesiastical pressures to conform to traditional patterns and to meet current expectations of institutional success. This freedom became real also because sufficient funds were made available to undertake a wide range of experiments, and because, in its search for faithful patterns, the staff was given the freedom to fail many times while seeking one "wineskin" that might be useful, not only in East Harlem but for the whole church.

This freedom is also reflected in the members of our churches. They, too, come from a wide range of religious traditions, or often from none at all. As families of God in East Harlem, for example, these congregations have no choice but to seek willingly for ways of worship that express their faith, but which at some point or another strike each person as strange or confusing. Because no one tradition dominates, we must find patterns in worship into which meaning can be poured and which will speak of the Gospel in terms that come alive in our situation.

Such freedom is, of course, a very dangerous business if there is not some clear locus of authority beyond what people like or are willing to try. We have sometimes used our freedom to do foolish things and have made many mistakes. But where our faith has come alive in worship and action, the patterns almost always turn out to be firmly imbedded in the traditions of the Reformation, and seem to parallel closely the life of the New Testament churches. At our peril we fail to take with utter seriousness the concrete glimpses we do have of life in the early church. The "new wineskins" turn out to be very old; they just have not been used for quite a while! They seem to make sense when they remind us who we are: a family of God's people, gathered together for worship, study, fellowship, and prayer, and then sent forth on his mission of service and witness in the world.

THE EAST HARLEM COMMUNITY

East Harlem is clearly defined by geography. Just north of 96th Street, the New York Central Railroad tracks emerge under Park Avenue and run on a trestle to the 125th Street station. Where the trains emerge from the tunnel, the wealth of Park Avenue, in one block, gives way to the slums of East Harlem. On the west, the boundary is Central Park; on the east, the river; and on the north, 125th Street. Here in a little over one square mile live approximately 185,000 people, a polyglot mixture, but roughly 40% American Negro, 40% Puerto Rican, and 20% remnants from all the previous immigrant groups.

The whole of East Harlem was built after 1890 really as a slum, that is, as tenements to house as cheaply as possible the immigrants who were flooding into America. It is an economic ghetto, a community which has poverty as its common denominator. Everyone comes to live here with great dreams of making his way upstream in American life. But especially for the most recent newcomers, American Negroes and Puerto Ricans, too often the dreams have died amid the sordidness and discrimination they find in a big city. Here in their most brutal forms they face all the grim problems of modern urban culture: racial discrimination, inadequate housing, broken families, over-crowded schools, juvenile delinquency, alienation from meaning in work, problems in the use of leisure time. In large measure the people of East Harlem feel the ultimate weight of all the forces which tend to make life impersonal and to destroy any sense of individual worth and dignity.

And in all of East Harlem, in 1948, there was not a single church of a major denomination ministering to the people of the community. Here, in the midst of great human need, in a radical mission situation, God's church clearly belonged.

The East Harlem Protestant Parish, begun in the late spring of 1948, was a concerted effort on the part of a group of Protestant denominations, in unity, to return to their mission in the inner city.

THE GATHERED LIFE OF THE CHURCH

We have come to understand the life of the Christian as existing in two areas; in the gathered life of the church, where Christians meet for their life together of prayer, study, worship and fellowship, and in the dispersed life of the church, that is, scattered abroad in the world as servants of Jesus Christ and witnesses to his kingdom.

In our gathered life we have tried to learn what it means to be a family of God's people. By such effort we come to see the church as persons, not as an institution, and we are concerned with relationships, with faith and love and witness. To become a family, to discover the unity which Christ grants to his people and which transcends all differences of race and class and education, we must spend time together. This takes two forms in our Parish.

The Bible Study Groups. Over the past five years, we have developed a pattern of Bible study that has become one of the two foci of our gathered life. Aware of our almost total ignorance of the Bible, we determined to begin a long-term, systematic attempt to know Scripture as a familiar landscape. The basic tool for Bible study is a Parish *Lectionary,* a little booklet published quarterly, following the church year. One passage is selected for study each week, often working in consecutive order through a biblical book, but at other times following a major theme and drawing each week on a relevant passage from the whole Bible.

On one evening of the week, usually Wednesday, all members of the Parish are urged to attend Bible study groups meeting in various apartments throughout the community.

In these sessions, the usual method is simply to read the Bible passage aloud and let Scripture raise its own questions in the minds of the group. When a clergyman opens the discussion with a critical explanation or spends time indicating the "crucial issues" to be considered, the meeting simply turns into a classroom, with teacher and pupils. When the clergy permit the group to hear and study the passage without introducing their ideas, the result is usually a lively discussion during which people really come to grips with the need to understand the meaning of the passage in its biblical context and to wrestle with its relevance for their own situation. The clergyman in this kind of give-and-take can have a real teaching role, but now he also stands together with the rest of the group under the issues which Scripture raises, rather than intruding his ideas between the group and the Bible. The evening sessions are scheduled for an hour and a half, but rarely does the group finally break up in less than two to three hours. There is often a strong sense that in our time together we have been truly blessed with the guiding, chastening, inspiring presence of the Holy Spirit.

The study on Wednesday night prepares for the Sunday morning preaching. On Sunday, one of the Scripture lessons and the sermon are based on the text studied during the previous week. The Reformation tradition—that the congregation must be alert to see that the true and lively word is faithfully preached—can take on reality and new meaning when the people have themselves studied and pondered the passage.

Corporate Worship. On Sunday morning when the congregation gathers for corporate worship, it is in a very real sense the in-gathering of Christ's soldiers from the front lines where they have been engaged in his work during the week. This is an essential focus for the gathered life of the congregation. The liturgy is really a drama in which the people, including the minister, engage in a common service involving four fairly distinct acts.

1. *Reporting.* The service begins with hymns and words of praise as God's people give thanks for his continual protection and care and express their gratitude for their safe return to the center of their nurture and preparation. This is followed by the act of confession—a confession that is designed to remind us all of the very real sins and transgressions which have been committed in seeking to be faithful during the past week. This is followed by the *Kyrie* and pardon, following which the whole congregation unites in saying together Psalm 23, or some other appropriate passage from Scripture that can serve as words of assurance.

The heart of this first act is called the concerns of the church. It begins when the minister is standing in the midst of the people and asks them to report on what has been happening in the week past in their mission in God's world. This is far more than a fancy name for a time of renouncement. A woman stands and asks for help in securing signatures on a petition demanding better police protection. Another urges all of us to register so we can vote in the coming election. A man tells about an important meeting for parents that will be held several days hence at a local school. Then the clergyman asks for the names of those who are sick and in trouble in order that the whole congregation may join in prayers for them. Others may ask for prayers on an occasion of joy, recovered health, or return of loved ones, or perhaps of an anniversary. The minister then kneels in front of the communion table and, informed by the people, prays for the specific issues which engage God's people in their life as Christians in the world.

2. *The True Life in Light of the Word of God.* The second act provides the occasion for listening to God's word as it comes to the people from the Holy Scriptures. Here we

listen again to God's word and ask for his direction in our personal lives, but more importantly in our mission in his world. After an Old Testament reading there is a psalm, often sung, and then a New Testament passage. These are taken from the weekly lectionary that has been studied by many of the congregation during the preceding week.

Directly following the Scriptures, the minister carries the Bible to the pulpit as a sign that his primary commission is to break open the word of Scripture that has just been read. Preaching in the Parish is thus thoroughly biblical, seeking always to relate the passage to the immediate demands of the world. We seek, in other words, to declare the secular relevance of the word of God.

3. *The Celebration of the Lord's Supper.* Communion is now celebrated each Sunday in the worship life of the full congregation. Here the family gathers together to be reminded of what their work and life is all about. This act begins with a sign of our fellowship, derived from the early kiss of peace, during which we shake one another's hands and sing an appropriate hymn. Then the elements of bread and wine, which are placed on the table near the door before the service, are brought forward, along with the offering of money. On behalf of the congregation, one of the elders offers a prayer.

As much of the symbolism as possible is that of a family festival—a time when aunts, uncles, cousins, and friends gather to celebrate a special occasion. The minister breaks the big loaf of Italian bread, quoting the words of Paul, "Because there is one loaf, we who are many are one body for we all partake of the same loaf." Then the bread is passed from hand to hand and each person breaks off a piece. Then the whole family eats together, remembering that we are united again to Christ and to one another and are given the food of life that we might enter into God's work. Here is truly a sign of the truth of the Gospel that in Christ there is neither rich nor poor, male nor female, bond or free, Puerto Rican, Negro, white—that at this moment in history we know the joy of his unity which transcends all human barriers.

4. *Sent Back in Mission.* The conclusion of the service is a strong reminder to return to our places of mission in the world. The congregation repeats the words that Jesus read in the synagogue, now called our Parish Purpose:

> The Spirit of the Lord is upon me because he hath anointed me to preach the Gospel to the poor. He hast sent me to heal the broken-hearted, to preach deliverance to the captives and recovering of sight to the blind, to set at liberty those that are oppressed, to proclaim a year when men may find acceptance with the Lord. Amen.

Having worshiped together in order to lift up our life and concerns to God and fed by word and sacrament, we are called to return to the world as the locus of our obedience. If we are to continue in Christ, we must look for signs of his presence in the world, seeking there to continue his ministry in service and witness. This is the task for which God has claimed the Christian. Our purpose is strengthened by a benediction such as this:

> Go forth into the world in peace; be of good courage; hold fast that which is good; render to no man evil for evil; strengthen the faint-hearted; support the weak, help the afflicted; honor all men; love and serve the Lord, rejoicing in the power of the Holy Spirit. And the blessing of God Almighty, the Father, the Son and the Holy Spirit, be upon you, and remain with you for ever. Amen.

Essential Reality of Corporate Worship. If it is imperative to see corporate worship as a reflection of the commitment of Christians to serve the world (and we thus consider the elements of worship as related at every point to the apostolate), it is also clear that corporate worship must also be seen under the rubrics of congregational participation. The essential character of worship, as the action not simply of the clergyman, but of the whole people of God, must be rediscovered and appropriated. At this point in history, the East Harlem Protestant Parish has given attention to this point by seeking to dramatize in every way possible the reality of the congregation as a family, drawn together as one body by Christ's love, and requiring that all members of the family participate fully when the family gathers for the celebration of word and sacrament.

Something of the element of participation can be seen in our use of the church year as a way of helping people participate in the liturgy through *recalling* the events of faith. Thus Advent Sunday is our New Year's Day, celebrated with a parish-wide service. All during Advent, we use a liturgy based on the earliest extant Advent litany, expressed also in the verses of the hymn, "O Come, O Come, Emanuel." Each week we hang a brightly colored "Great O" in the chancel as a mobile, with a symbol in the center of the "O," suggesting a way in which we await Christ's coming. Thus we seek to recapture again the same sense of expectancy and longing that characterized the life of Israel and is so well expressed in the Advent texts from Isaiah.

Participation is also *re-enactment*. Maundy Thursday has become for us the point of primary re-enactment in learning what it means to celebrate the Lord's Supper. We try as closely as possible to relive the actions described in the gospels. The pews at the front of the church are removed and long tables put in their place. In the early evening the congregation, including children, gather for a fellowship meal of bread—the long loaves of Italian bread common to East Harlem—wine, and fish. We sing hymns spontaneously and talk during the meal. Following the supper, one of the clergy simply stands at his place at the tables and preaches a brief sermon. The text is customarily the foot washing passage and is used to speak about the servanthood of Christ. The minister reminds the congregation that the stole he wears is also his only symbol of authority, that of a servant.

Following the sermon, the congregation come forward in groups of eight and stand on the steps of the chancel while the clergy kneel down and, using the ends of their stoles, wipe the shoes of each person. Then several of the elders receive the people's offering and bring it forward to the communion table, along with a loaf of bread and pitcher of wine from one of the supper tables. The whole congregation joins them in large circles around the table, just as a family might come to a banquet meal, and just as Jesus sat around the table with his disciples. Then the words of institution are read, the elements are consecrated and the communion is celebrated, following as closely as possible the biblical account. The elements are passed from hand to hand, with the people holding the bread until all have received some, and then eating together.

This kind of re-enactment means that on the next communion Sunday, when the congregation is again invited to gather around the table, many will recall with understanding the meaning of their actions.

It is easy to overstate the case and to expect too much from the forms of our worship. But if worship is to open channels of God's grace, certainly we must begin by understanding what we are doing and learn to enter as active participants into the actions of the liturgy. Participation, beyond the important elements of recall and re-enactment, also involved for us simply providing as many opportunities as possible for the congregation to enter actively into the service. They are encouraged to say "amen" at the end of all prayers, and are given many responses, prayers, the creed, and the Parish Purpose to speak.

But the essential element in participation is the creation of a sense of authentic involvement of the *whole congregation as a family,* bound together more truly by Christ than with their own flesh and blood. This is the miracle which faith proclaims at the communion table.

But in our day we have lost much of the meaning of this sacrament of the common life of Christians. In the inner city (and I suspect in most churches in America) you can presuppose no biblical literacy whatsoever. People literally do not connect the communion service with the Last Supper. Worse, the symbols we use in the usual communion service, and even the mechanics of it, say all the wrong things about what we are doing to people who are not versed in Scripture and for whom communion is a new and strange experience. We use funny little pieces of bread or queer wafers, unlike any other food we ever eat; the table is far removed from the congregation, or is inconspicuous, or has become an altar. All this suggests that the service is some kind of magic, or an esoteric rite, when in fact it is the ordinary bread of life we should break at a family banquet table. The infrequency of celebration suggests it is something special, when in fact it must be normative and natural and central. And communion has become a private and personal matter, even in those churches where people come forward to a rail. In fact it is corporate, the family meal of God's people.

Perhaps all this is inevitable when, as Christians, we do not gather as those who come to a family meal, knowing each other as brothers. When men and women do not know in their own lives the meaning of human brotherhood and family love, there is little reality in the symbol of the table where we gather in fellowship to celebrate the mighty acts of God. In a word, integrity in communion demands that those who gather at the table must be a family, united in Christ, not as a theological fact alone, but as a reality that is expressed in the common life of the community. It also demands that those who gather at the table know what they are doing and in very truth are re-enacting the meaning of the Lord's Supper.

Integrity in communion implies that the family of the church must spend time together in order that the reality of our unity in Christ may be discovered and that we may learn what it is that sustains our life as a community of grace. The insistence upon the participation in a Bible study group each week has provided the basic structure through which we may come to know each other as brothers. In a Bible study group some time ago we were studying 1 Corinthians, wrestling soberly and almost in despair with the problems of immorality in the church at Corinth. I was sitting in the room with a man who was then living with a woman other than his wife, with a woman who was having another child out of wedlock, and all of us together were forced to expose our lives and ourselves to the judgment of God's word. This kind of continual week-after-week meeting, standing together under the Scripture enables us to know one another—that is to say, it almost forces us to open our lives to other people and to dare to expose who we really are. We learn the joy of speaking the truth in love, and even harder, of accepting the truth, spoken to us in love. I am beginning to suspect that the primary channel through which the Holy Spirit comes to us is our brothers, and only through this kind of exposure in depth is the Holy Spirit really able to speak to us with power.

Then, when the community gathers, the congregation comes forward to receive the communion, gathering in large circles around the communion table. There we look at each other, not as strangers, but as those who have come to know one another in depth and love. Men and women who, when you first met them, shook hands but did not look you in the eye, now look at you, and there is joy and love in their hearts. When we reach the act of fellowship before coming to the table, all the people present turn around and shake hands with each other as a sign of the brotherhood that is becoming a symbol with a new meaning.

In one sense, the congregation at worship is a secular event. Here men seek not to escape from the world into a religious place, or to engage in peculiar actions of some strange cult, or to achieve righteousness against an evil world. Rather, when at a communion table all sorts and conditions of men are freely welcomed, when Negro, White and Puerto Rican break bread as guests of their one Lord, they proclaim a truth of profound secular relevance. In a world that no longer quite believes that racial and class barriers can be shattered, the church bears witness to the fact that in Christ all men are made brothers, all distinctions shattered. All men must live in some form of community. The Christian seeks simply to reveal for all nations the form of community which God intends for all men. At the Lord's table, we seek to define the nature of true human life together.

CONCLUSION

In the midst of the failures of the old patterns in East Harlem, we have been driven to look for the gifts of God to the life of his church, the new community which stands against the mass community of modern life. In the face of utter depersonalization, the church must become again a family. God is indeed renewing his church when he calls forth a community of faithful people who find that their life together is the means of restoring them to their true humanity in the midst of great unhumanity. The struggling churches of our Parish are no success story, but they have pointed us to the reality of God's church. Again and again, we have seen half dead symbols of our faith come alive again, heard the word preached with power, felt the presence of Christ at his table, and shared in the miracle of rebirth. His gift is this: that in his church he does bring forth among us a community of saints who believe in the channels of grace and live in and through them. We can only pray that in our freedom to seek new patterns of worship we shall learn to listen and to obey God, for surely he is here among the needs and problems of our community, calling us to join Christ who is always to be found wherever there is poverty and blindness and captivity and oppression.

The Eucharistic Sacrifice
and the Real Presence

MAX THURIAN

It is possible to speak of the Eucharist as a sacrifice within the context of the biblical conception of the memorial.

The Eucharist is a sacrifice for three reasons:

1. It is the sacramental *presence* of the sacrifice of the cross, by the power of the Holy Spirit and the Word, and it is the liturgical *presentation* of the Son's sacrifice by the church to the Father, in thanksgiving for all his blessings and in intercession that he may grant them afresh.

2. It is the *participation* of the church in the intercession of the Son before the Father in the Holy Spirit, that salvation may be accorded to all men and that the kingdom may come in glory.

3. It is the *offering* which the church makes of itself to the Father, united to the Son's intercession, as its supreme act of adoration and its perfect consecration in the Holy Spirit.

This sacrificial understanding of the Eucharist, in the light of the biblical memorial, provides a basis for a Christian definition of sacrifice:[1] *sacrifice is an act of presentation of*

---

1. E. Masure, *Le sacrifice du chef* (1957), pp. 31-51, has attempted a definition in terms of "transference of property" or "return to God" in two stages: surrender and gift. His very broad definition turns sacrifice once more into an action of "humanity before God" (p. 49). It does not seem possible to provide a definition of sacrifice in general and then fit the Eucharist into this category; rather the attempt has been made to start from the biblical memorial and to discover, in the light of this, the meaning of the Eucharist and define Christian sacrifice.

a reality to God, for the purpose of a blessing upon that reality or upon him who presents it.

Thus, in the early church, *sacrificium* denoted not only the expiatory sacrifice of Christ but everything offered to God—the offertory at the Eucharist, the Eucharist as a whole, the eucharistic elements, the spiritual offering (confession of faith, charity, repentance, humility, prayer, fasting) and liturgical offices in general.[2] The Bible, in its conception of the memorial, provides the basis for these different uses of the sacrificial idea. Whatever the act of sacrifice, it is expressed in Hebrew by the Hiphil of the verb *qarab,* i.e., *hiqrib,* which corresponds in Greek to προσφέρω, and in Latin to *offero,* and means to make approach, to present or carry before. Hence at the consecration of the Levites, which is assimilated to an offering, Moses "presents" *(hiqrabta)* them before the Tent of Meeting, before the face of Yahweh, and the children of Israel lay their hands on them and "Aaron shall offer the Levites before the Lord for a wave offering,[3] on the behalf of the children of Israel" (Num 8:9-11). The verb generally denotes the act of presentation (Ex 29:3; Lev 1; 2:12; 8:21; Num 7:2, 10; Hag 2:14; Ezra 8:35; 1 Chron 16:1; 2 Chron 35:12, etc.). It expresses the initial and fundamental action, both material and spiritual, of the sacrifice, which consists in *presenting* or bearing before God a being or thing in praise or supplication for the purpose of a blessing. The corresponding Greek and Latin terms (προσφέρω, *offero*) have the same meaning: to bear or carry before. This is the very essence of sacrifice, being its initial and basic movement.

2. A. Blaise, "Sacrificium," *Dictionnaire latin-français des auteurs chrétiens,* p. 731 f.

3. A wave offering was that part of the sacrifice which belonged to the priest; it was waved over the coals of the altar to signify that it was given to Yahweh, and returned by him to the priest (Ex 29:26). The Levites were given as a wave offering to God and so to the people.

A general definition of sacrifice can be drawn from the Eucharist as a memorial in the biblical sense, and this definition shows that the essential action of Christian worship is at one with basic human nature. Nevertheless the Eucharist as a sacrifice is uniquely original. The offertory, the church's offering, is an act of presentation of a reality to God for the purpose of a blessing upon that reality. The church presents the bread and the wine that they may be blessed; it presents the gifts that they may become signs of brotherly charity; it presents itself that it may be sanctified. In this sense, the Eucharist is a sacrifice which resembles those of the old covenant and even those of human beings in general. It is the finest and noblest sacrifice that man has ever offered; it is the sacrifice of praise, which, according to rabbinic tradition, could be offered only in the messianic era. Yet, despite its spiritual character, this sacrifice is primarily a human act which cannot itself claim to please God, in view of the sin and misery of those who offer it. And it is at this point that the complete originality of the eucharistic sacrifice becomes apparent. Christ himself, through the Holy Spirit and through his word ("This is my body . . . This is my blood"), makes up what is lacking in the poverty-stricken offering of the church; he substitutes himself for the church's miserable sacrifice. In the eucharistic prayer, the church does not offer a mere human reality; it is enabled to present to the Father, along with its own poverty-stricken offering, the unique and perfect sacrifice of Christ. The glorified Lord takes up into his heavenly intercession the poverty-stricken sacrifice of Christians and it becomes rich with the riches of Christ and acceptable, because carried by the Son into the heavenly sanctuary. The originality, value and effect of the eucharistic sacrifice lie in the fact that through it the church is able to present a perfect offering, the cross of Christ, which allows access to our offerings, prayers and praises, and makes them acceptable, however poor they may be and however miserable are those who present them.

The term "sacrifice" as a designation of the Eucharist is very important, because it recalls the fact that only the sacrifice of the cross and the heavenly intercession of Christ can make our own sacrifice, thanksgiving and intercession acceptable. Even the expressions "sacrifice of thanksgiving" or "sacrifice of praise" can suggest that our thanksgiving and our praise have some value in themselves, and those who make use of them, for polemical purposes, against the doctrine of the Mass, are not always aware that by using them they are in danger of arriving at exactly the opposite conclusion to that which they desire. To avoid or to combat ideas of repetition of or additions to the sacrifice of Christ, they entertain the idea of a Christian sacrifice which is a simple response to the divine gift. But we are not only incapable in ourselves of giving anything of value to God, because of our sin; we are also incapable of responding to his gifts as we should, because of our weakness. God has to give us the will, the joy and the power to thank him, to pray to him and to love him as we should. The Holy Spirit must inspire us to utter praise and he must put upon our lips the word of God. That is why the psalms have such an important place in the liturgy. Only Christ can offer a true and acceptable sacrifice, and this is precisely what the Eucharist signifies. When we call the Eucharist a sacrifice, in the sure faith that there is only one true sacrifice, that of Christ, we declare thereby that it is impossible for there to be any acceptable human sacrifice, and that in the Eucharist the church presents the unique sacrifice of Christ, which alone gives meaning and value to our worship and to our charity.

From the sacrificial aspect, the Eucharist is the liturgical presentation of the sacrifice of the Son by the church to the Father. But the church can perform this action of presentation only because the sacrifice of the cross is sacramentally present in the Eucharist through the power of the Holy Spirit and the Word. It is this point that must be first considered.

THE SACRAMENT OF THE SACRIFICE

It is evident that the sacrifice of Christ on the cross is alone an expiatory sacrifice. It alone has expiated our sin before God and produced the complete reconciliation of humanity with God; it alone has accomplished the eternal redemption of the faithful by God. From his ascension to his return, Christ presents this redemptive sacrifice in the heavenly sanctuary in intercession, that its effect may be applied to each man. The Eucharist then, which is a sacramental presence of the sacrifice of the cross and a liturgical presentation of that sacrifice to the Father, is not an expiatory sacrifice, but the sacramental means whereby the Father, hearing the joint intercession of the Son and of the church, applies salvation to all men in order to hasten the manifestation of the kingdom. Baptism is the decisive beginning of this application, while the word and the Eucharist continue its completion.

Every expression that may impair the uniqueness of the redemptive sacrifice of the cross and of the heavenly intercession of Christ should be avoided when speaking of the Eucharist, while at the same time the sacrificial reality of the Eucharist must not itself be impaired. This careful balance of the doctrines of mediation and of the sacrament has not always been preserved in theological circles.

Calvin strongly criticized the sacrificial character of the Eucharist, according to the popular medieval idea of repetition, but he affirmed the unity of the sacrifice of the cross and of the Eucharist. "The bread is his *body*. For we have it for this reason, that it may be a covenant in his body, i.e., a *covenant* which has been once for all ratified by the sacrifice of his body, and is now confirmed by eating, viz. when believers eat that sacrifice . . . For the blood was poured out to reconcile us to God, and now we drink it spiritually in order to have a share in that reconciliation. Therefore, in the Supper we have both the covenant and a reinforcing pledge of the covenant."[4]

Calvin saw in the Eucharist, as in the sacrifice of the cross, a ratification of the new covenant with God. By the Eucharist we participate in the reconciliation of the cross and are confirmed in the covenant; the Eucharist includes both the covenant and its renewal in us. The unity of the cross and the Eucharist is thus clearly emphasized; the cross is present in the Eucharist as a covenant with God. Calvin, it is to be noted, saw this unity in the act of communion. For him the Eucharist necessarily involved the communion of the faithful by means of which they participate in the reconciliation of the cross, receive the covenant and are confirmed in it. We have already seen that Calvin considered the fraction to be a sign of Christ's sacrifice: "we come to enjoy through it a share in redemption and the application to us of the benefits of his sacrifice . . . the Supper is a mirror which represents Christ crucified to us."[5] But when he saw the sacrifice of the cross in the Eucharist, he always thought of the Eucharist as communion. His opposition to the sacrifice of the Mass was largely due to the great number of Masses at which there was no act of communion. He would not admit that "by their daily offering the blessing of redemption is brought to the living and the dead" when "a person eats it on his own."[6] But two pages below, speaking of the fraction

---

4. See *The First Epistle of Paul the Apostle to the Corinthians*, trans. J. W. Fraser (1960), p. 244 ff.

5. *Ibid.*, p. 248.

6. *Ibid.*, p. 244.

and the communion, he uses the same terms in order this time to approve of them: "the benefit of the sacrifice is applied to us." There is no doubt that non-communicating attendance at the sacrifice of the Mass played a great part in Calvin's criticism of the sacrificial character of the Eucharist. In a sermon of 1558,[7] he gives his interpretation of St. Paul's saying concerning the blessing of the cup (1 Cor 10:16). It is particularly striking that he upheld the blessing of the cup itself: "For St. Paul does not say that thanks were given with the cup, nor does he say the cup by which blessing is given, but he says that the cup is blessed." This blessing indicates that the cup is "dedicated" to certify to us "that our Lord Jesus Christ gives himself to us and that the blood which he once shed for our redemption has become the means of our washing and that our stains are purged away by it before God."

Again there is this repeated emphasis upon the unity of the cross and the Eucharist. Christ gives himself to us, and his blood shed once for all our redemption thereby becomes the means of our purification before God. Both the redemption of the cross and its present power of purification are certified to us in the Eucharist. The word "certified" is not to be understood simply in its cognitive or intellectual sense; it expresses the certainty of faith which is attached to the reality and presence of Christ and of our purification before God through the mystery of the Eucharist.

Calvin goes on to define even more clearly participation in the sacrifice of Christ in the Eucharist: "The cup and also the bread must be sanctified in accordance with this practice, in order that the wine may be a figure[8] of the blood of our

7. *Sermon 7 on 1 Corinthians.*
8. The word "figure" does not involve a watering down of the idea of the real presence, rather it expresses the outward appearance of the sign and its inner reality, which is the body and blood of Christ. The same word *figura* was used by the Fathers (Tertullian, *Adv. Marc.,* IV, 10: *"Hoc*

Lord Jesus Christ and the bread of his body, in order to show that we have truly fed upon him, and being as it were grafted into him may have a common life, and that by the virtue of the Holy Spirit may be united to him,[9] in order that the death and passion that he has undergone may belong to us and that that sacrifice, by which we are reconciled to God, may be attributed and imputed to us now as if we had offered it ourselves in person." By the Eucharist we appropriate the death and passion of Christ, and his sacrifice on the cross, which has reconciled us with the Father, is "attributed and imputed" to us now, as if we had offered it ourselves. The sacrifice of Christ becomes our sacrifice in the Eucharist. The presence of the sacrifice of the cross in the Eucharist could not be better expressed.[10]

The cross is a unique sacrifice in the order of *expiation, reconciliation* and *redemption*. The Eucharist is a sacramental sacrifice in the order of *application* of salvation (remission of sins) based upon the unique expiation, of

---

est corpus meum dicendo, id est figura corporis mei"; Ambrose, *De Sacramen.,* IV. 5.21: *"quod est figura corporis et sanguinis domini nostri Jesu Christi."* For the words *similitudo, figura* and *antitypus* see A. Wilmart, "Transfigurare," *Bull. d'ancienne litt. et d'arch. chrétienne,* I, 1911, p. 280).

9. Note the demonstrative sense of the sacrament (*to show* that we have truly fed) and the effective sense (we *may have* a common life . . . we *may be united* to him).

10. In his *Short Treatise on the Lord's Supper,* Calvin expressed himself more categorically against the idea of sacrifice; but he was criticizing the Mass as "a sacrifice for acquiring the remission of sins," in the sense of a repetition of the cross. He accepted the idea of a representation of the sacrifice, as found in the Fathers, but rejected, as Judaic, a form of celebration which recalled only the old covenant. We do not offer or sacrifice, but "we take and eat that which has been offered and sacrificed." He even rejected the idea of the "application of the unique sacrifice" which he was prepared to admit in his *Commentary* on 1 Cor 11:24. But the center of his attack was the Mass without communion, which was in danger of appearing to be a repetition of the unique sacrifice of the cross and not a participation in the unique sacrifice and an application of the sacrifice of redemption.

communion based upon the unique reconciliation, and of *intercession* based upon the unique redemption. The Eucharist as the sacrament of the unique sacrifice of the cross applies salvation (remission of sins) to each person, and this was obtained once for all by the expiation of Christ and maintains communion between God and men, which was re-established once for all by the reconciliation of Christ, and unites the intercession of the church to the heavenly intercession of Christ which was inaugurated once for all by Christ's work of redemption.

Without taking anything from the uniqueness of the cross, the expiation, the reconciliation, or the redemption, the Eucharist is the sacrament or the presence of the unique sacrifice continuing in the church today the application of salvation and communion with God, together with the intercession of Christ.[11] The Eucharist is the cross present in the church and extending the unique and perfect work of Christ to all men in space and time and in depth. In the Eucharist, the church meets Christ who applies salvation to each one, deepens the communion of men with God, intercedes for all and hastens the coming of the kingdom.

The Eucharist is the sacrament of the real presence of Christ; it is the sacrament of the sacrifice of the cross, "for

11. The perfecting of the redemption in each one of us through the Eucharist is expressed liturgically in the Latin prayer at the offertory (*secreta*) for the ninth Sunday after Pentecost: "Grant unto us, O Lord, to participate in the mysteries as is fitting, for each time we celebrate the memorial of the sacrifice (of Christ), the work of our redemption is accomplished (*exercetur*), through Jesus Christ, thy Son, our Lord." *Exercetur* is rich in meaning. It may be rendered "is accomplished," "performs its action" or "is kept in movement"; each translation asserts the permanence and presence of redemption. Cf. O. Casel, "Beiträge zu römischen Orationen. Die Sekret vom 9. Sonntag nach Pfingsten im römischen Messebuch," *Jahrbuch für Lit. Wis.*, XI, 1931, pp. 35 f. Some Protestant eucharistic hymns give clear expression to the presence of the remission of sins in the Eucharist, e.g. *Louange et Prière*, 1957, No. 206: "By the blood that thou hast shed, my sins will be forgiven."

the Lord does not offer his body to us, just his body with nothing else said about it, but his body as having been sacrificed for us."[12] And the presence of him that was crucified is not that of an inert victim, but of the lamb as slain and living in heaven, continually presenting his unique sacrifice in intercession for all men.

The sacramental presence of the sacrifice of the cross is accomplished by the power of the Holy Spirit and of the Word. No action of the church can be conceived as taking place outside the work of the Holy Spirit, and no liturgy can omit reference to him. The real presence of Christ and of his sacrifice in the Eucharist is a fruit of his word: "This is my body . . . This is my blood," but this word is not a magical formula which produces its effect by recitation. It is the Holy Spirit who gives life to that word and makes it present in the sacrament celebrated by the church. Without the Spirit active within the church, that word is a dead letter. A true celebration of the Eucharist is a celebration in the Holy Spirit and in the church with the word of Christ. This means that the eucharistic liturgy should include the words of institution and an invocation of the Holy Spirit. Moreover an essential relation must be seen between the liturgy of the sacrament and the liturgy of the word, which together form a unity. The word of God, proclaimed in the readings and in the preaching, affects the Eucharist, properly so called, through the power of the Spirit. The word of God, read and preached, acts on the church through the Spirit and consecrates it to meet Christ in the sacrament. This consecration is necessary because a Eucharist celebrated by an unworthy community, not consecrated by the word and the Spirit to discern the Lord's body, would be a scandal and a condemnation of that community. Both the Holy Spirit and the

---

12. *The First Epistle of Paul the Apostle to the Corinthians,* trans. J. W. Fraser, 1960, p. 248.

word are essential to consecrate the church for the Eucharist. The readings and the sermon are thus integrated with the liturgical action as essential elements. This integration of the word of God in the eucharistic prayer is strongly emphasized in those prefaces which pick up the theme of the lessons, especially of the gospel. This relation of gospel and preface has already been noted, particularly in the Ambrosian rite. A suitable formula of introduction to the biblical readings, in the spirit of this consecration for the Eucharist, would be, for example:

> Come, Holy Spirit of truth:
> Lead us into all truth.
> Lord, consecrate us in the truth:
> Thy Word is the truth (Jn 16:13; 17:17).

THE PRESENTATION OF THE SACRIFICE

The Eucharist is the liturgical presentation of the sacrifice of the Son by the church to the Father. This is the sense in which we have understood the Eucharist to be a memorial. Several liturgical types of the Old Testament, such as the *memorial* of the oblation, and the incense, the *presentation* of the shewbread, and the *mercy-seat* by the ark, are considered as symbols of this liturgical presentation.[13] This

---

13. I am in agreement with Douglas Jones ("Anamnesis in the LXX and the Interpretation of 1 Cor 11:25," *Journal of Theological Studies,* VI (1955), pp. 183-91) when he notes the flexibility of the biblical use of the word memorial, *anamnesis* or *mnemosunon*. Nevertheless it does seem to me that he has inadequately related this term to the more general framework of liturgical piety and prayer both in the Old Testament and in Judaism. In particular, he passes too quickly over the case of Cornelius (Acts 10:4, 31) where the term memorial, *mnemosunon,* is given its full liturgical meaning and has Jewish piety as its context. While I admit the flexibility of the term, it does seem to me that the word, understood in the context of Jewish piety—as in the account of Cornelius —has a quite natural meaning, viz. to recall to God, by an act of praise and prayer, what he has done once for all, and to present what the believer has done as an offering and a prayer.

Douglas Jones seems disturbed by those writers who accord the word

liturgical presentation is the action of *recalling* to God the Father the sacrifice of God the Son, eternally present, acceptable and effective before him through God the Holy Spirit; it is the act of *placing* the sacrifice *before* him, of *stirring up* his pity.

The Protestants of the sixteenth century considered that the doctrine of the sacrifice of the Mass impaired the uniqueness of the sacrifice of the cross for the remission of sins, and they opposed a popular heresy to the effect that Christ died for original sin while the Mass is offered for present

---

"memorial" a primarily sacrificial meaning. In this I am in agreement with him. The twofold meaning of the word must be emphasized, in that it can mean both a recalling to men and a recalling to God, in praise and supplication. When it is applied to the Eucharist, the term means first of all the presence of the divine activity on behalf of his people, as a recalling to the believer, and the presence before God of what he has done in the course of the history of salvation, as a recalling in praise and supplication. The term memorial also has a secondary meaning which refers to the sacrificial understanding of the Eucharist. It does not have this as its primary meaning, but when it is used of the Eucharist it shows how and in what sense it can be conceived as a sacrifice, i.e. only in the sense that it is an act of proclamation, a memorial before men and before God, a presence and an actualization of the unique sacrifice of Christ.

Douglas Jones tends to consider the Passover as no more than a looking backwards, a remembering of the past. But the Passover is an actualization of the work of salvation and in this sense it is an act of proclamation before men and an act of praise, as well as of supplication, before God. As already stated, this understanding of the Passover provides the Eucharist with its proper sacrificial meaning. It would, however, be a wrong method of approach to affirm first of all, on the basis of an ecclesiastical tradition, that the Eucharist is a sacrifice, and then go on to discover a biblical foundation for this. This has not been my line of approach. I began by considering the Eucharist within the context of the Passover and of the memorial, and it was precisely because of this that I was led to a new definition of the conception of sacrifice which is Christian, eucharistic and fully biblical. It is because the Eucharist is the presence of Christ's sacrifice as a memorial that it is a sacrifice at all, but with a new and proper meaning.

Douglas Jones's objection, based upon the danger of seeing the church's liturgy as an act of mediation, is overcome if the idea of the presence of Christ's work is central in our understanding of the Eucharist. It is not by any act of mediation on the church's part, offering a new sacrifice, nor by the mediation of the believers' memory, remembering the work of

sins. Catholic theologians equally opposed this heresy in the *Confutatio pontificia* which was a reply to the Confession of Augsburg.[14] The pontifical theologians expressed the unity of the cross and the Mass, and the uniqueness of Christ's sacrifice, in this manner: "He offered himself once on the cross with the outpouring of blood; he offers himself now in the Mass as in a peaceable and sacramental sacrifice. Once he offered himself by suffering the passion in a visible form, now he offers himself in the Mass without suffering the passion under the veil of the mysteries."[15] The parallelism and contrast of the words used provides the key to the doctrine of these theologians. On one side, the unique outpouring of the blood, on the other the peaceable and sacramental sacrifice; the reference to the peace offering of the old covenant is to be noted, and this was not a sacrifice for sin, but a communion sacrifice expressing the community of life

---

Christ on the cross, that the saving activity is applied now to the people of God and to the world. Just as Christ once for all took the place of every human good work when he *alone* accomplished the work of our salvation, so also in the Eucharist, by the sacramental presence of his unique sacrifice, without any act of mediation by the church, except for its word and actions, the Lord takes the place of every liturgical *work* that he may be the only priest, the only agent in the liturgy, in the church and before the Father. As I have already said, this sacrificial interpretation of the Eucharist as a memorial emphasizes the unique present mediation of Christ, our only intercessor. It is still his unique work of salvation, his sacrifice on the cross, which is our prayer and praise before God. Neither prayer nor praise are responses possible to the church on its own, but they are indeed his response which he gave once for all on the cross, and which he continues to give on our behalf and in us to God the Father, in his heavenly intercession, which is sacramentally present in the Eucharist, the memorial of thanksgiving and intercession.

14. *"Hoc nunquam auditum est a catholicis, jamque rogati plerique constantissime negant ab eis sic doceri."* *Confutatio pontificia,* II, 3, ed. C. A. Hase, *Libri symbolici Ecclesiae evangelicae,* 1846, pp. LXXIV-LXXVIII. The same refutation appears in *Responsio privata Colcheo-Vesaliensis,* cited by H. Lammer, *Die vortridentinisch-katholische Theologie,* 1958, p. 272.

15. *"Semel oblatus est in cruce effuso sanguine; hodie offertur in missa ut hostia pacifica et sacramentalis. Tunc offerebatur passibilis in forma visibili, hodie offertur in missa velatus mysteriis impassibiliter." Ibid.*

between the faithful and God (Lev 7:11-16). The term *hostia sacramentalis* also emphasizes the uniqueness of the cross and its sacramental presence in the Eucharist. The adjective "sacramental" applied to the sacrifice expresses, as commonly in theology, the presence of an historical saving event in a mode which is both eschatological and belonging to the church. It expresses the presence of the salvation accomplished by Christ in the church, his body, as a hidden anticipation of the kingdom which is to come. The opposition of terms in the *Confutatio pontificia* is to be understood in this eschatological sense: *in forma visibili,* in a visible form . . . *velatus mysteriis,* under the veil of the mysteries. John Eck, one of the defenders of Catholicism, expressed the same doctrine of sacrifice in this way: "If it may be said that Christ's offering is twofold . . . there is one by which he offered once his living body and his blood to God the Father on the altar of the cross . . .; but there is another, the sacramental offering, by which the church daily offers Christ through the priests in the sacrifice of the Mass . . . as a memorial *(in commemorationem)* . . . of the first offering accomplished once upon the cross."[16] Elsewhere he wrote: "Christ made his offering once on the altar of the cross and its effect flows to us each day."[17] This image of a river, whose source is the cross and which flows to us through the Eucharist, is very suggestive and safeguards both the uniqueness of the sacrifice of the cross and the possibility of a sacramental sacrifice.

16. *Enchiridion,* loc. XVII, 1537, p. 194 f.
17. *Ibid.,* p. 196. Cf. the views of numerous Catholic theologians in the sixteenth century, Jean Colchée, A. de Castro, Cajetan, etc. (*D.T.C.,* X, 1, 1104-1109). Cajetan, *Opuscula,* 1582, II, p. 231, wrote: "The difference is in the mode of offering, for once he offered himself bodily, now he is offered spiritually. Once he offered himself in the reality of death, now he is offered in the mystery of death." The same distinction and unity is emphasized by the opposition of the terms *corporaliter . . . spiritualiter, in re . . . in mysterio.*

The idea of the presentation or showing forth in the Eucharist of the unique sacrifice of Christ is found in certain Catholic theologians of the period between the beginning of the Reformation and the Council of Trent. According to John Eck: "The priest, in the name of the church *(in persona ecclesiae)*, presents to God the Father the offering accomplished by the Son on the altar of the cross and offers himself."[18] According to John Gropper: "The church exposes *(proponit,* places before) or re-presents *(repraesentat)* Christ before God the Father."[19] In view of this one wonders why Catholics and Protestants were unable to agree on this essential aspect of the Eucharist. Calvin could condemn as "a mere quibble" the statement that "the Mass is not a new sacrifice, but only an application of the unique sacrifice."[20]

Reformed theologians from the end of the sixteenth century were more willing to consider this proposition, e.g., Philippe du Plessis-Mornay in his treatise *De l'institution, usage et doctrine du saint sacrement de l'Eucharistie, en l'Eglise ancienne,* 1598;[21] Edmé Aubertin, pastor at Paris, in his patristic "summa," *L'Eucharistie de l'ancienne Eglise,* 1633,[22] and above all Pierre du Moulin, minister of the Reformed Church at Paris, in his celebrated *Bouclier de la foi ou défense de la confession de foi des Eglises Réformées*

18. *Ench.,* loc. XVII, p. 195.

19. *Antididagma,* 1544, fol. 63, Vᵒ.

20. *Short Treatise on the Lord's Supper* (J. K. S. Reid, *Calvin: Theological Treatises,* 1954, p. 156).

21. Philippe du Plessis-Mornay was a politician, not a pastor. His work was printed by Jerôme Haultin of La Rochelle.

22. This was a work of considerable length which surveyed patristic thought in the first six centuries, in reply to Bellarmine, Du Perron and others. It was printed by Pierre Aubert at Geneva and comprises 660 pages plus Index. It indicates the concern of Reformed theologians in former days to base their theology on patristic teaching, which was to them an authoritative guide to the interpretation of the Bible. E. Aubertin is very liberal with regard to the term "sacrifice," much less strict and severe than Calvin and more ecumenical, like all Reformed theologians in the seventeenth century.

du Royaume de France, contre les objections du Sieur Arnoux, Jésuite, 1635.[23] This book, though apparently concerned with polemics and apologetics, is very ecumenical in what it has to say of the Eucharist. "How and in what sense the Eucharist can be called a Sacrifice," is the title of Section CLVII:[24]

"The holy scriptures use the term sacrifice of alms, prayers, a contrite and humble heart, martyrs, ministers of the gospel, and in general of all sorts of good works. But there are particular reasons for calling the Eucharist a sacrifice:

"I. Because this sacrament was instituted to proclaim the Lord's death until he come (1 Cor 11). Hence the Eucharist may be called a sacrifice, since it represents the sacrifice of the Lord's death. According to the principle that signs and representations ordinarily take the name of that which they signify.

"II. It may be said that in the Eucharist we offer Jesus Christ to God, insofar as we ask God to receive on our behalf the sacrifice of his death.

"III. The Eucharist is a sacrifice of thanksgiving for the divine benefits and especially for the benefit of our redemption through Jesus Christ.

"IV. The early church had a particular reason for calling the Eucharist a sacrifice, for it was the custom for each believer to bring his gifts and presents to the table, and part of this was used for the Eucharist, while the rest was food for the poor. These presents were called sacrifices and oblations . . ." (There follows a number of patristic quotations.)

"However, there may be two kinds of sacrifice: the one propitiatory and redemptive, the other eucharistic and

23. This work was also printed by Pierre Aubert at Geneva. For the literature in general see R. Snoeks, *L'argument de tradition dans la controverse eucharistique entre catholiques et réformés français au XVIᵉ siècle,* 1951.

24. *Op. cit.,* p. 629 f.

expressive of thanksgiving. The Eucharist is a propitiatory sacrifice insofar as it is a sacrament and a commemoration, in the same way that the cup is the covenant, the bread is the body of Christ and circumcision was the covenant with God, or as the rock from which the waters flowed was said to be Christ. But strictly speaking, the Eucharist is a sacrifice of thanksgiving; it is, as the canon of the Mass states, *sacrificium laudis,* a sacrifice of praise. Hence the Fathers used the term Eucharist, i.e., thanksgiving.

"There is no reason to think it strange that one and the same action should be called sacrament and sacrifice. For between a sacrament and a sacrifice there is the same difference as between taking and giving. Thus the Eucharist may be a sacrament insofar as by it God gives us and conveys his grace, and a sacrifice insofar as we offer him our praise and thanksgiving."

Also worthy of quotation is the conclusion of section CLVIII, "The Belief of the Ancients touching the Sacrifice of the Eucharist." Pierre du Moulin mentions Peter Lombard and Thomas Aquinas and asserts that truth compels both the opponents and upholders of the Reformation to speak in similar terms: "In short, truth is so strong that our opponents, outside the heat of debate, usually say the same things as we do. If you read Lombard, *Sentences,* Book IV, Distinction 12 G, or Thomas Aquinas, *Summa,* Part III, quaest. 83, art. 1, you will see that they are in complete agreement with us and that they maintain that the Eucharist is called a sacrifice solely because a commemoration is made of the sacrifice of the cross and the sacrifice of the Lord's death is applied to us that we may be partakers of its benefit."

The ecumenical spirit of this passage is to be particularly noted, in that it recognizes a general agreement between opposing theologians when they are "outside the heat of debate." Du Moulin then considers that the Eucharist may be called a sacrifice insofar as it is (i) a representation of Christ's sacrifice; (ii) a memorial-offering of Christ to God; (iii) a thanksgiving for redemption and other divine gifts; (iv) the offertory of the church through the gifts of the believers. The second point is particularly interesting from the pen of a Reformed theologian and it exactly expresses what I have defined by the word "memorial." I should hesitate to use the verb "to offer," and would prefer "to present" so that the expression would not conflict with our contemporary theological language. "It may be said that in the Eucharist we offer (we present) Jesus Christ to God, insofar as we ask God to receive on our behalf the sacrifice of his death." Du Moulin also notes the two kinds of sacrifice: "the one propitiatory and redemptive, the other eucharistic and expressive of thanksgiving." It might have been expected that he would refuse to apply the first to the Eucharist and would accept only the second. But he accepted the term "propitiatory sacrifice" upheld by the Council of Trent: *"Sacrificium visibile esse propitiatorium pro vivis et defunctis."*[25] For him "the Eucharist is a propitiatory sacrifice insofar as it is a sacrament and a commemoration," i.e., the propitiatory sacrifice of the cross is sacramentally present in the Eucharist under the form of a memorial. The term "sacrament" signifies the actual presence of the propitiatory sacrifice of the cross, and the weaker term "commemoration" no doubt denotes the symbolism of the Eucharist in that it is a rite which figures the sacrifice of Christ. Today we should say that the Eucharist is a sacrifice insofar as it is a sacrament and a symbol, making the sacrifice present sacramentally and representing it symbolically.

Du Moulin then gives some examples: the Eucharist is the sacrament and commemoration of the propitiatory sacri-

25. *Sessio* XXII, *c.* 2.

fice in the same way that the cup is in relation to the new covenant, the bread in relation to the body of Christ, circumcision in relation to the old covenant and the rock in the desert to Christ. These examples are not of course to be ranged all on the same level, but they do explain in what sense the Eucharist is to be understood as the sacrament of the propitiatory sacrifice: there is a presence of the reality in the sacrament, in such a way that the sacrament may be said to be the reality which it presents and represents, as the cup *is* the new covenant, and the bread *is* the body of Christ, circumcision the old covenant, and the rock Christ. Finally, du Moulin seems to check himself a little when after all he expresses a preference for the term "sacrifice of thanksgiving" or "sacrifice of praise" *(sacrificium laudis)*. This passage is to be seen as a real ecumenical *tour de force* somewhat hedged in through prudence ("But strictly speaking . . ."). Nevertheless his ideas cannot be denied, and du Moulin has left us a traditional conception of the Eucharist as a sacrament and a sacrifice: a sacrament because in it we take what God gives; a sacrifice because in it we offer our praise and thanksgiving and "offer (present) Jesus Christ to God, insofar as we ask God to receive on our behalf the sacrifice of his death." This is precisely what I mean by "the memorial of thanksgiving and intercession."

In connection with this understanding of the sacrifice of the cross "proposed, exposed, presented and offered" to the Father in the Eucharist, we may quote a theological poem, written by the seventeenth-century Reformed writer Ogier de Gombaud, who died sometime after 1666. This poem is not concerned with the Eucharist, but it shows how the believer, incapable of offering anything of value, takes refuge in the unique sacrifice of Christ and presents it to the Father. Thus, although it concerns Christian sacrifice in general, this poem may be applied to the Eucharist, in the spirit of a Philippe du Plessis-Mornay or a Pierre du Moulin:

> Evil subdues me, and so great my woe
> When sin, for all my struggle, wins the day,
> That in this dark abyss I cannot know
> What homage to my Maker I should pay.
>
> I long to offer what thy law commands,
> My prayers, my vows, my fruit of faith to thee,
> But—since my heart deserves not thy demands—
> Christ is my offering, for eternity.
>
> Accept thy Son, O Father: see that cross
> Whereon, to pay the utmost that I owe,
> In blood and death He yields thee all His loss;
>
> And by His love's abundance I implore
> No longer, Lord, thy right of justice show,
> But shed thy pity, now and evermore.[26]

In the eighteenth century, in an attempt to further unity with the Church of England, Father Le Courrayer published a *Dissertation sur la validité des ordinations des Anglais et sur la succession des évêques de l'Eglise anglicane.*[27] He was attacked for his ecumenical zeal and so, in 1725, he issued a *Défense de la Dissertation sur la validité des ordinations des Anglais.* It must be acknowledged that he was mistaken in separating the doctrine of the eucharistic sacrifice from that of the real presence and in affirming that Catholics and Anglicans could agree on the first without being united on the second. Nevertheless, his conception of sacrifice is very interesting, in that he wished to be faithful to Trent and at the same time shared the conception of those seventeenth-century Reformed theologians whose works have been quoted. "The Council," he says, "calls the celebration of the

---

26. Quoted by A. M. Schmidt, "Les poètes calvinistes français des origines à la révocation de l'édit de Nantes, témoins d'une vie théologique," *Revue Réformée,* IV, (1950), p. 274 f.

27. Published in French at Nancy in 1723.

Eucharist a sacrifice, *ut Ecclesiae relinqueret sacrificium,* because, since the sacrifice consists in the offering of a sacrificed victim and since the passion of Christ is always present, every time that this victim is offered, the sacrifice of Jesus Christ is offered. . . . But the sacrifice is not renewed, for Jesus Christ dies only once. Nor is it a sacrifice which is continued or supplemented, since it had its perfection and completeness in the death of Christ. It is rather a sacrifice which is represented, *quo cruentum illud semel in cruce peragendum repraesentaretur;* a sacrifice recalled, *ejusque memoria in finem usque saeculi permaneret;* and a sacrifice applied, *atque illius salutaris virtus applicaretur.* There is therefore in the Eucharist a true sacrifice, in the sense that there is therein made to God the oblation of a death which is always present, *mortem annuntiabitis.* But as this death is not repeated, this sacrifice is no more than the representation of another one, *Hoc facite in meam commemorationem* . . . There is no question here of simply recalling Christ's death to remembrance, but of the offering of that remembrance to God in order that in virtue of what he has suffered he may have pity upon us."[28]

Father Le Courrayer was rightly criticized for separating the doctrine of the eucharistic sacrifice from that of the real presence, but his understanding of the sacrifice as a memorial-offering is quite in line with the biblical concept of the memorial, as well as with the thought of du Moulin, and therefore has a place in any ecumenical discussion of the Eucharist. His views have been quoted here to show that when Protestants and Catholics, like du Moulin and Le Courrayer, seek to rethink the doctrine of the eucharistic sacrifice in an ecumenical context, they reach positions which are very close to each other. . . .

28. *Op. cit.,* IV, *c.* 4, p. 157 f.

The Reformed Church has always been concerned to preserve belief in the real presence; thus, in 1931, the Synod of the Reformed Churches of France declared:

"As concerning the mode of the Lord's presence in the sacrament, believers can have different views, but they cannot differ on the fact of the presence itself; it is a real presence according to the Spirit and is inseparable from the elements of the Eucharist in the very act of celebration."

The Eastern Orthodox, more than Western Christians, have had this respect for the mystery of the real presence without attempting to overdefine its mode. Before the sixteenth century, the majority of Orthodox theologians wisely refused to advance beyond a simple belief in the real presence and the idea of a change of the bread and wine into the body and blood of Christ, without defining this change in philosophical terms. Some, who had read St. Thomas, introduced the idea of transubstantiation, but without explanation or illustrations to make it easier to comprehend. After the sixteenth century three tendencies may be noted: i) that which retains the idea of transubstantiation; ii) that which accepts the doctrine of Trent, without explaining transubstantiation; iii) that which is content to affirm the reality of the presence, while rejecting even the idea of the permanence of the accidents.

It is to be noted that all these tendencies, eastern or western, have a close connection with the different Christological positions adopted and the different conceptions of the relation between the two natures. Those who have a tendency to separate the humanity and divinity (a Nestorian attitude) also have a tendency to separate the bread from the body and the wine from the blood of Christ and find it difficult to express the connection between the eucharistic elements and the person of Christ. In the fourteenth century, Timothy II, a Nestorian patriarch, expressed himself thus:

"This bread and this wine, which are not by nature either body or blood, are called by the grace of the Holy Spirit which is poured upon us body and blood of Christ . . . Since we say that the bread and the wine are body and blood by grace, it cannot be supposed that they are God by nature."[29] Those who have a tendency to confuse the humanity and divinity (a Monophysite attitude)[30] also have a tendency to confuse the bread and the body and the wine and the blood, by refusing to maintain even the Catholic distinction between the substance which changes and the accidents which persist. In this connection, as with Christology, the teaching of Chalcedon should be respected. Although the substance of the Eucharist, its basic reality, is the body and blood of Christ, its chemical nature remains bread and wine, and we cannot define the mode of their relation, which is, however, such (as the Scriptures compel us to acknowledge) that the Eucharist *is* the body and the blood of Christ.

THESES CONCERNING THE REAL PRESENCE

1. The body and blood of Christ, his whole humanity and deity, are truly, really and substantially present in the Eucharist.

This real presence of his body and blood is the presence of Christ crucified and glorified, here and now, under con-

29. *De sacramentis,* ed. Assémani, *Bibliotheca orientalis,* III, p. 294 f.; W. de Vries, *Sakramenten Theologie bei den Nestorianern, Orientalia Christiana analecta,* 133 (1947), pp. 214-220. Nestorians always find it difficult to separate ideas of substance and nature from their concrete manifestations. Nestorians at the present day adhere to the orthodox doctrine; see *D.T.C.,* art. "Eucharistie," col. 1322 ff.

30. W. de Vries, *Sakramenten Theologie bei den syrischen Monophysiten, Orientalia Christiana analecta,* 125 (1940); I. H. Dalmais, "Note sur la théologie des Mystères dans les Eglises Syriennes (occidentales et orientales)," *Maison-Dieu,* 19, p. 60 f.: "There is present . . . the ancient semitic conception of holiness as a quasi-physical fluid which may be communicated by touch."

crete signs. The meaning of every corporal presence is to attest concretely the presence of that person that he may enter into a concrete communion. By the real presence of his body and blood, the church knows that Christ is there concretely in the midst and it receives him by means of a concrete sign. The substantial presence of Christ does not denote a material presence, in the natural sense, but the presence of the profound reality of the body and blood of Christ crucified and glorified.

2. Christ glorified sits at the right hand of the Father in his humanity and in his deity; how it happens that he is also present corporally in the Eucharist is a mystery and the work of the Holy Spirit which the church cannot define.

The real presence of Christ is not to be understood as a localization limited to the elements of bread and wine; Christ cannot be shut up within the limits of the created world. But the bread and the wine at the Eucharist do become a privileged place where Christ himself, in his humanity and deity, may be met and received. Christ glorified, by his power to subject all things, acts through the Holy Spirit and by his word on the bread and the wine, to make them into a place where the church may meet him and receive him corporally, so that they are the instruments through which the church can reach him in the fullness of his humanity and deity.

3. Christ then, through the Holy Spirit and his word, takes sovereign possession of the elements of bread and wine, draws them to himself and assumes them into the fullness of his humanity and deity, in such a way that they become truly, really and substantially his body and blood.

The glorified Christ takes the bread and wine as a sign to manifest his corporal presence in the church. The bread and wine of the Eucharist are no longer ordinary bread and wine. Of course their chemical nature remains that of bread and wine, but behind this faith must recognize the true and new substantial reality of the bread and wine: the body and blood of Christ. The church does not limit itself to the bare fact of the reality of the bread and wine; it also believes that they are changed, not chemically, in the sense that the glorified Christ takes possession of them to make them a concrete sign of his presence in our midst, to make them his body and blood, a place where he may be found locally, contemplated sensibly and communicated concretely.

4. It is the Holy Spirit, requested of the Father, and the word of Christ, uttered by the church, in the course of the memorial performed in the great eucharistic prayer, that make the bread and the wine the body and blood of Christ.

It is not necessary to determine the precise moment at which the mystery is accomplished. It is by means of the whole liturgical action, and especially by the whole eucharistic prayer (from the *Sursum corda* to the *Amen*) that the bread and wine are eucharistized by the Holy Spirit and the word of Christ, in the memorial presented to the Father. In the unfolding of the liturgical movement a privileged moment at which consecration is effected is not to be selected nor must a tension be created between the words of Christ and the invocation of the Holy Spirit. The normal liturgical order would be for the Holy Spirit to be invoked before the words of institution to signify that he gives them life and actuality, in such a way that they become the Lord's body and blood. A second epiclesis or invocation may have its place after the words of institution and the anamnesis, but in this instance they prepare the congregation to receive the body and blood of Christ. Two such invocations are to be found in the old Alexandrian liturgy of St. Mark.

5. The figure of the bread and the wine is the sign that Christ is our sustenance; this sign of bread and wine is the vehicle of the real presence of the body and blood of Christ

in us. This real and corporal presence should be contemplated and received in the liturgical action when Christ acts with and for us and gives himself to us in communion.

The Eucharist is not a sacred object, but an action and an act of communion. The signs of bread and wine are eucharistized for the sacrifice of thanksgiving and intercession, which are accomplished in the communion. The sick, who desire it, though they are kept at home, are associated with the eucharistic action; communion may be carried to their homes by what is to be regarded as an extension of the celebration.

6. The body and blood of Christ which are objectively present in the Eucharist for communion really come to those who receive them: to those who have a right intention as a means of sanctification, and to those who will not recognize the body of Christ, through lack of faith, and the body of the church, through egotism, as a means of condemnation.

St. Paul expressed the objectivity of the eucharistic presence of Christ when he pointed out the grave consequences of an unbelieving or egotistical act of communion, without discerning the body of Christ or the body of the church by faith and love (1 Cor 11:27-34). Where there is an unworthy act of communion, he who lacks faith and love meets Christ, really present, but does not receive the fruits of this encounter: on the contrary he is condemned for the absence of faith and love.

7. After the celebration has been completed by the communion of the faithful, including that of the sick in their homes, the real connection between Christ and the elements left over is a mystery that should be respected.

Since the conclusion of the Eucharist is the communion ("Take, eat . . . Drink ye all of this"), we cannot define the nature of the relationship of Christ and the elements that remain after the completion of communion. There is no need to speculate about the continuance nor about its disappearance. The mystery is to be respected. Because of such an attitude of respect, it is fitting that the eucharistic remains should be consumed after the celebration.[31] Negligence in this matter tends to compromise belief in the real presence, whereas a balanced respect is a sign of true belief in the presence of the body and blood of Christ and a sign that, at least, the material basis of this presence has a right to our respect. Belief in the efficacy of the word of Christ involves belief that it will not leave unchanged those created things upon which it comes.

8. Communion in the body and blood of Christ is at the same time a communion of each individual in the body of Christ, the church. United in Christ in one offering by the church, the faithful are joined indissolubly together by communion in the body of Christ.

If the church makes the Eucharist, the Eucharist makes

---

31. Only sufficient wine for the communion should be consecrated; where an insufficient amount has been consecrated, then more wine should be added to the chalice while it still has some eucharistized wine in it, and this will safeguard the centrality of the eucharistic prayer. Such a practice has its basis in tradition. When the congregation was very large, it was impossible to consecrate all the wine necessary on the altar. The celebrant consecrated only his own chalice and, before communion, the deacons consecrated the chalices for the congregation by adding a little of the wine consecrated by the celebrant or a fragment of consecrated bread. The prayer in the Roman rite: *Haec commixtio et consecratio,* was thus understood literally. Besides, *Haec* replaced a primitive *fiat* after the Council of Trent; thus the meaning of the prayer was: "May the mixture and consecration of the body and blood of our Lord take place." The three signs of the cross made with a particle of the host over the chalice recall this primitive form of consecration; the priest drops the particle into the wine and this is an action which no longer has any meaning in terms of consecration. This complex rite has other origins, but here it is sufficient to note the primitive idea of consecration by mixing a fragment of consecrated bread (or a little consecrated wine) with the wine intended for the communion of the faithful. De Jonge, "L'arrière-plan dogmatique de la commixtion," 1953, quoted by T. Maertens, "L'histoire de la communion au service de sa pastorale," *Paroisse et Liturgie,* 1958, No. 5, p. 352.

the church. The Eucharist unifies and joins together the members of the body of Christ; those who have been baptized are joined together in unity and can but seek the deepening, extension and fulfillment of their unity. As the sacrament of unity, the Eucharist is the sacrament of charity which it supports and extends. Hence, in the quest for the unity of the church, intercommunion should be seen not as an end but as a means of recognizing and living the fact that Christ establishes the unity of his body in the communion of his eucharistic body. And in the life of a local community, the Eucharist is the place where the church is built up and deepened in charity. That church which celebrates the Eucharist frequently beholds Christ, through the Eucharist, developing his charity, his unity, and making his word and his life effective in the world.

The Passover of Christians

ROGER GREENACRE

It was because of God's love for us that Christ came into the world. From all eternity the love of God the Father had been poured out in the Holy Spirit upon the Son and returned by the Son in the Spirit to the Father. Christ's coming into this world was in order that mankind might be incorporated into his humanity and so "through him, with him, and in him"[1] be carried up in the movement of his love and in the power of the Spirit to the Father. He came into this world, therefore, solely in order that he might return to the Father, but return bringing redeemed humanity with him. Because he came into a world of sin to unite to himself a humanity in the grip of sin, this return could be no peaceful journey, but a passover of mortal conflict with the powers of darkness.

This passover wrought by our Lord in his own person (for he was utterly alone as far as any human support was concerned) was the unique and final passover in the sense that the work of redemption effected by it has a final, once-for-all, finished quality. It is unrepeatable, and yet it is constantly at work to effect our own passover so that we may follow our Lord through his passion and death to rise with him and sit with him and reign with him. Yet this passover of ours is in no sense independent of or distinct from Christ's passover; it is part and parcel of it. St. Paul can speak of the action of God in raising Christ from the dead and his action in raising

1. From the concluding doxology of the Canon of the Roman Mass.

102

us up to newness of life as one single movement, as one single
action: "But God, who is rich in mercy, out of the great love
with which he loved us, even when we were dead through
our trespasses, made us alive together with Christ (by grace
you have been saved), and raised us up with him, and made
us sit with him in the heavenly places in Christ Jesus" (Eph
2:4-6). To understand this identification we need to return
once more to what St. Paul says about Baptism in the epistle
to the Romans.

> Do you not know that all of us who have been baptized into
> Christ Jesus were baptized into his death? We were buried there-
> fore with him by baptism into death, so that as Christ was
> raised from the dead by the glory of the Father, we too might
> walk in newness of life.
> For if we have been united with him in a death like his, we
> shall certainly be united with him in a resurrection like his.
> We know that our old self was crucified with him so that the
> sinful body might be destroyed, and we might no longer be
> enslaved to sin. For he who has died is freed from sin. But if
> we have died with Christ, we believe that we shall also live with
> him. For we know that Christ being raised from the dead will
> never die again; death no longer has dominion over him. The
> death he died he died to sin, once for all, but the life he lives he
> lives to God. So you also must consider yourselves dead to sin
> and alive to God in Christ Jesus (Rom 6:3-11).

It is in this passage more clearly than anywhere else in the
New Testament that we are confronted with the identification of the Christian with Christ precisely in the act of his
passover—his *transitus*—by the way of the cross to the glory
of the resurrection. It is on the paschal character of Christian baptism that this view of the Christian life as a passover
is founded.

In examining this passage the first thing to note is that,
whatever variations there may have been in early baptismal
practice, St. Paul's language is inspired by the symbolism of

immersion, in which the function of the water is not so much to cleanse (though elsewhere Paul can speak of Baptism in terms of washing) as to drown. Baptism, in the vivid phrase of Norman Nicholson, is "birth by drowning"[2] and has behind it the experience of the Israelites in the Red Sea and the exodus which our Lord had to accomplish at Jerusalem and which he spoke of as his baptism. So it is that St. Paul can speak of the Israelites as having been "baptized into Moses in the cloud and in the sea" (1 Cor 10:2) and the Prayer Book Baptism service can include a prayer which speaks of God's leading the children of Israel through the Red Sea, "figuring thereby thy holy Baptism." The developed ceremonial of the baptismal rites of the early church made the link with our Lord's own death and resurrection even more striking and explicit. The candidates descended to the font, stripped off all their clothes, faced west to renounce the Devil, were immersed three times in the waters, then ascended from the font towards the east, were anointed, clothed in white robes and given lighted candles.[3] Moreover, all this took place, if possible, in the night of Easter: the catechumens celebrated their own death and resurrection in the celebration of Christ's death and resurrection.

Yet St. Paul is obviously not speaking of a merely symbolic act but of a real identification with Christ's death and resurrection. Christ's death marked the moment of his victory over the powers of evil; death could no longer have any dominion over him for he was at this moment freed from all the limitations and humiliations imposed upon him by his

---

2. *Birth by Drowning* is the title of a verse-play by Norman Nicholson (London: Faber & Faber, 1960), telling the story of Elisha and Naaman the leper. "As you deduce," writes Mr. Nicholson in a private letter, "the phrase refers, by implication, to baptism, though this is not specifically the subject of the play."

3. The handing over of a lighted candle is later than the other ceremonies; it is first recorded in the eleventh century.

identification of himself with our humanity in its fallen state of lowly weakness. Death was for him the gateway to his glorification. So too our identification in baptism with the death of Christ is not an identification with the physical act of disintegration but with the act in which our Lord renounced and triumphed over the old Adam, liberating the human race from the grip of the powers of sin and death. And as our identification with his death is not a literal anticipation of the moment of our own physical death, neither is our identification with his resurrection a literal anticipation of the moment of our bodily resurrection, but an identification with his resurrection as the creative act by which God renewed the human race in exalting and glorifying his Son and in pouring out his Holy Spirit. If St. Paul can quote Psalm 2: "Thou art my Son, today I have begotten thee" as a reference to the resurrection (Acts 13:33), so there is a sense in which we can apply it to ourselves as a reference to our baptism.

However if we confine ourselves to seeing our own passover in terms of baptism alone we shall never make sense of it. First of all we have to link Baptism with Confirmation and First Holy Communion in a unified movement of Christian initiation. The essence of this movement is what St. Paul calls a *translation*. God, he says, "has delivered us from the dominion of darkness and transferred us ["translated us," *A.V.*] to the kingdom of his beloved Son, in whom we have redemption, the forgiveness of sins" (Col 1:13-14). Every other aspect of baptismal grace—forgiveness, regeneration, the conferring of character—must be seen in the light of this movement in which we are so completely identified with Christ as to be incorporated into the body of his risen and glorified humanity, identified with him moreover in his own passage through darkness to light, in his death and resurrection. It is not that our baptism places us immediately into a state of perfection and easy security where we have no need to fight and no risk of falling, but that it unites us with Christ so that in the victorious power and energy of his risen life we may continually live out our baptism by being conformed to Christ in his warfare against evil and in his death to sin and by being transformed by the new life of his resurrection.

The fourth gospel records that from the side of the crucified Christ on Calvary there came out blood and water. It is no extravagant fantasy that led the Fathers to see here the signs of Baptism and the Eucharist, both of which receive their efficacy from the cross and both of which unite us to the mystery of the cross. For if we are united once for all to Christ in his death and resurrection by being grafted through baptism into his body the church, this union is kept in being and constantly renewed and strengthened by the Eucharist. The Eucharist no less than Baptism is a paschal sacrament for it is the sacrament of the unity of the body of Christ with its glorified and ascended head, the memorial of the cross and resurrection, the new passover banquet, the sacrifice of praise. As a sacrifice it is in no sense independent of or additional to that of Calvary; it is identical with it, for it exists to bring us into vital contact with the once for all event of Christ's death and resurrection.

If we consider the significance of what our Lord did and said over the bread and wine on the night before he suffered, we shall see that first of all he plainly declared his coming death to be a sacrifice, with his body being given and his blood being poured out for the forgiveness of sins and for the inauguration of a new covenant, a radically new kind of relationship between God and man. By his words and actions he not only declared his death to be a sacrifice; he also solemnly consecrated himself to that sacrifice, acting both as priest and as victim. But our Lord went one step further, for he gave the bread and the cup to his disciples, commanding them to eat and to drink. By this he was drawing his disciples into the closest association with his sacrifice; for by continuing to "do this" through the ages they were not only communicating in the fruits of his oblation but in the very act of oblation itself.

If we ask who it is that offers in the eucharistic sacrifice we do not have to make a choice between saying either that it is Christ or that it is the church; similarly, if we ask who or what it is that is offered in the eucharistic sacrifice we do not have to choose between Christ and his church. The Eucharist is precisely the sacrament of unity, of the unity of head and members in one body; it is the sacrament of the whole Christ, *totus Christus*.[4] In the Eucharist it is the whole Christ that offers and the whole Christ that is offered, for it is the means whereby the barriers of time and space are transcended and Christians in every place and in every generation are incorporated into the movement of Christ's own once for all enacted self-oblation. At every eucharistic celebration we give ourselves to be laid upon the altar in our gifts of bread and wine; we give "ourselves, our souls and bodies"[5] to be offered in and with our gifts in sacrifice and thanksgiving to the Father; we give our lives for Christ to say over them, as over our gifts, "This is my body . . . This is my blood"; we give our lives to be broken, and shared, and given away. Both in consecration and in communion our lives are identified with the life of Christ and our offering of ourselves with Christ's offering of himself.

The Eucharist is the supreme link between Christ's sacrifice and the present life of the church—between his *transitus* and our own. The church has nothing of its own to offer but

4. The phrase is St. Augustine's: "This is the whole Christ: Christ united with the Church" (*In Ps. xc, Sermo 2*).

5. From the Prayer of Oblation in the Prayer Book Communion Service, cf. Romans 12:1.

the offering of Christ made once for all upon the cross and accepted and vindicated in the resurrection, and so it only dares to offer itself in and through its head and bridegroom and his perfected and unspotted sacrifice. So after every Eucharist we can say, in the words of the Liturgy of St. Basil—"Finished and perfected, so far forth as is in our power, is all the mystery of thy dispensation, Christ our God. For we have held the remembrance of thy death, we have seen the figure of thy resurrection, we have been filled with thine unending life, we have had fruition of thine inexhaustible delight: whereof be thou pleased that we all be accounted worthy in the world to come, by the grace of thine unbegotten Father, and thy holy and gracious and life-giving Spirit, now and for ever and world without end. Amen."[6]

So then a paschal character is given not only to our Baptism but to our eucharistic worship and through that to our whole Christian life. Death too, for the Christian, has a paschal character. "Physical death consummates sacramental death; it completes our incorporation into Christ in his redemptive act. The summit, as it were, of carnal man's weakness becomes, in his acceptance of it, the supreme means of being caught up with the Savior in his death and also therefore in his triumph."[7]

It is significant that St. Paul constantly writes of the Christian life not in terms of the cross alone, nor in terms of the resurrection alone, but in terms of both united together as a single mystery. "For his (i.e., Christ's) sake I have suffered the loss of all things, and count them as refuse, in order that I may gain Christ and be found in him, not having a righteousness of my own, based on law, but that which is through

6. *The Orthodox Liturgy* (London: S.P.C.K., 1939), p. 96.
7. F. X. Durrwell, *The Resurrection* (London: Sheed & Ward, 1960), p. 347.

faith in Christ, the righteousness from God that depends on faith; that I may know him and the power of his resurrection, and may share his sufferings, becoming like him in his death, that if possible I may attain the resurrection from the dead" (Phil 3:8-11). In these verses we see put in a nutshell the essential character of Christian living: it is knowing the fellowship of Christ's sufferings and the power of his resurrection. Again St. Paul tells us that "we are children of God, and if children, then heirs, heirs of God and fellow heirs with Christ, provided we suffer with him in order that we may also be glorified with him" (Rom 8:16-17); and earlier in the same epistle he refers to Christ as "Jesus our Lord, who was put to death for our trespasses and raised for our justification" (Rom 4:24-25).

There is a sense in which it can be said that we are still waiting for the final and definitive passover, which is the *parousia,* the return of Christ in power and glory. But if for the Jews in the Old Testament the true reality of the passover was all in the future, it is not so for us: we look back to the central act of history, no mere type or figure but the true substance of our redemption, and we look forward to our resurrection not as something set totally in the future but as something begun in us at our baptism. The new life, the new age of the Spirit, has already begun; so "we cleanse out the old leaven" (1 Cor 5:7) that we may celebrate the passover of unleavened bread in newness of life. That the new life has already begun, that our translation has already been effected, is the message of the Easter Day epistle: "If then you have been raised with Christ, seek the things that are above, where Christ is, seated at the right hand of God. Set your minds on things that are above, not on things that are on earth. For you have died, and your life is hid with Christ in God. When Christ who is our life appears, then you also will appear with him in glory. Put to death therefore what is

earthly in you . . ." (Col 3:1-5). The process of our sanctification is nothing else than the transformation and trans-
figuration of our lives by the paschal light of Christ. "And
we all," says St. Paul, "with unveiled face, beholding the
glory of the Lord, are being changed into his likeness from
one degree of glory to another" (2 Cor 3:18); "Beloved,"
says St. John, "we are God's children now; it does not yet
appear what we shall be, but we know that when he appears
we shall be like him, for we shall see him as he is" (1 Jn 3:2).

The holy week liturgy is concerned with the passover of
the Jews and with the passover of Christ. It is no less concerned with *our* passover, and it is engaged in the work of
effecting it through the ministry of the word and of the sacraments. "Cross and resurrection," writes the archbishop of
Canterbury, "are the ground of the church's origin, the secret
of the church's contemporary being, the goal of the church's
final self-realization on behalf of the human race. The word
and the sacraments in the midst of the church make known
to its members continually what is their origin, their secret
and their goal. For the *Word* is the Word of the cross,
whereby the church is made, renewed and judged. The
Eucharist is the proclaiming of the Lord's death until his
coming again; the setting forth before God and man of the
whole drama of his life, death, resurrection and parousia;
and the feeding of his people with his broken body and out-
poured blood."[8]

8. A. M. Ramsey, *The Resurrection of Christ* (Revised edition, Glas-
gow: Fontana, 1961), p. 97.

Worship and the Cross and Resurrection of Christ

HARALD RIESENFELD

The writings of the apostolic age provide surprisingly little information on worship in the early church. Of the rituals which may have existed—the forms were certainly by no means fixed—only fragments are left, some hymns and prayers, some baptismal formulas and not least the words of the institution of the Eucharist. It is not possible to set forth worship in the New Testament—as far as it is a matter of its outward shape—as a model for Christian worship throughout the ages. On the other hand, many passages in the New Testament bear upon the significance of worship, and that because Christian life and thinking were from the beginning concentrated upon worship as being in some way the form of human existence. This is why cultic terminology as such is frequent in the New Testament, a fact which points to a close connection between worship and the totality of Christian belief. In that setting the cross and the resurrection of Christ have a central position.

THE OLD TESTAMENT BACKGROUND

In order to understand the New Testament concept of worship it will always be necessary first to summarize what the Old Testament says on this subject. There is a straight evolution from the one to the other, and that is why the question

111

must be studied from the point of view of the major issue of the interrelation of the two Testaments, the dominant feature of which is the dialectical duality of continuity and new creation. The Old Testament, however, represents in regard to terminology and modes of thought a *praeparatio evangelica* of the cultic categories which form the basis of Christian worship.

Worship is a divine institution, given to the people of God. With a slight exaggeration it might be said that the Old Testament in its entirety circles around the problem of worship, not only because its writings have been constantly recited or sung in the services of the temple or the synagogue, but because they reveal a thorough-going theme: true and proper worship. God has chosen a people and established his covenant in order that the people should serve him. It is the duty of the servant to do the will of the Lord. Therefore God has given his law, which expresses two pairs of aspects which are essential for worship and can never be separated from each other: the cultic and ethical aspects on the one hand, and the personal and social aspects on the other, covering the whole complex of public and private functions in the life of the people: "You shall be holy; for I the Lord your God am holy" (Lev 19:2).

Worship implies atonement for sin and—through death— the gift of life. A dominating feature in Jewish worship was, however, the large altar in the main court of the temple, where burnt offerings were presented all day by priests and levites. This part of worship also had been prescribed by the law, and if some of the prophets criticized the lack of congruence between the devout attitude of the people offering sacrifices and their moral life (e.g., Amos 5:21-24), their critique did not aim at the abandoning of the sacrificial cult, which in itself was a divine institution. Sacrifices can be offered to God only because he has taken the initiative in providing the sacrificial cult.

Sacrifices create communion between God and mankind as well as between human beings. This aspect appears in the sacred meals. Sacrifices expiate sin which separates man from his Creator and causes the wrath of God. They renew holiness, which is the presupposition of the essential gift of God: blessing and life. The slaughter of the victim and the pouring out of its blood are characteristic points in the sacrificial cult, and the victim represents in a symbolic way the person of him who offers. The situation of man in relation to God is such that life cannot be given otherwise than through death.

Worship implies self-surrender as a condition of communion. When a man offers gifts or victims, they symbolize the offering up of his own person and of his life. This concept reaches its highest expression in the figure of the suffering servant (Is 52:13—53:12), who can be said to represent a synthesis of Jewish conceptions of sacrifice: it becomes clear that the way to blessing goes through atonement, the way to life through death, the way to communion with God and with men through self-surrender and self-sacrifice. It thus becomes evident that worship is not only an outward act, but involves the totality of a person's life.

Disintegrated worship still suffers from sin and therefore reaches neither full atonement nor full life. The failure of worship in Old Testament times was not primarily the lack of piety or of religious life. On the contrary, there was an intense religious activity going on throughout the history of Israel, continuing in the post-exilic period which coincided with the rise of the synagogue. Seen from the point of view of the New Testament, the failure was that in Old Testament times wholeness was lacking, the transformation of life into a unity of existence and service towards God and fellowmen. Sacrifices never ceased, but still no perfect expiation was established, festivals and life-giving rites were performed, and yet they did not create holiness and genuine life.

It was a demonstration of the fact that human worship is in no way sufficient. Even the enigmatic figure of the suffering servant was only a myth or a prophecy—or probably a combination of these two—but it still lacked reality.

THE WORK OF CHRIST

During his earthly life, Jesus was perfectly loyal to the cult of his people. But at the same time it became apparent, through his sayings and through the symbolic actions which he performed, that the time of the temple was limited and that a new worship was to take its place (e.g., the plucking of the ears of corn, Mk 2:23-28; the cleansing of the temple, Mk 11:15-17). During a few days the outlines indicated by these prefigurations were filled with substance. When Jesus held the last meal with his disciples, when he went to Gethsemane and Calvary to suffer and to die, his words and actions became worship in the true sense of the word (e.g., Jn 17). The cultic forms developed in the Old Testament finally revealed their true sense in the light of what the Lord did in the upper room and on the cross, when he represented in his own person the suffering servant and the paschal lamb, the priest and the victim, God and man, and thus achieved true worship. As a consequence he could rise on Easter morning from the dead to the fullness of life and to heavenly worship.

The interpretation in cultic terms of the cross and the resurrection is certainly not the only one which can be given of these central acts of redemption and re-creation, but it is vital and indispensable. In the person of Christ and in his life and redemptive work, true worship became a fact and a reality, conceived and achieved by God through his Son.

Christ's worship was performed in perfect obedience to God's will. The difference between the worship of Christ and that of the Old Testament lies in the wholeheartedness of the earthly life of Christ in obedience to God and in serving his fellow-men. The possibility as well as the effect of such a perfect obedience is to be considered from the point of view of the incarnation. There is also the question of the intention in the mind of Jesus. Is it not the early church which has interpreted the person and work of Jesus in categories taken from the Old Testament worship? The answer is that sayings of Jesus which surely are authentic, give witness of the way in which Jesus himself interpreted the meaning of his life and his death. The sayings about the son of man are consistent with the whole earthly ministry of Jesus and in them the idea of worship is evident (e.g., Mk 10:45).

Worshiping his Father, Christ went through death to life. The narrative of the temptation (Mt 4:1-11) demonstrates the insight that the kingdom of God—and that means the fullness of life as well as the fullness of worship—cannot be established by other means than by the death of Christ. Jesus was tempted to provide acceptable conditions of life for the human race by mere power, but he was conscious, already in the beginning of his ministry, of the fact that the problem of life cannot be solved apart from the problem of worship. Atonement was necessary in order to make obedience and devotion possible. The results of the self-surrender of Jesus, accomplished in his death, were anticipated during his ministry in the devotion and mutual service practiced in the inner circle of his disciples and among those who followed him, and furthermore, in the miracles in which the qualities of full and perfect life became manifest.

The Last Supper and the institution of the Eucharist provide another clue to the interpretation which Jesus gave of his death (e.g., Mk 14:22-25). The sacrificial aspect becomes evident in the words "poured out for many." Moreover, the bread and the wine symbolize the separation by death of the body and the blood. But as the slaughter of the victim confirmed the covenant of Mount Sinai, so the voluntary death of the son of man established the new covenant, resulting in the newness of life. Thus bread and wine are at the same time symbols of life.

The self-surrender of Christ has effected communion. The effect of the obedience of Christ in his death, which led on to the resurrection, is shown by what Christian doctrine calls his exaltation to the right hand of God: "Therefore God has highly exalted him . . ." (Phil 2:9). In his heavenly glory, Christ has entered into still closer communion with his Father. Because of his obedience, he was installed in the function of high priest of the heavenly worship and received from his Father the promise of the Holy Spirit (Acts 2:33) to be given by him to human beings on a scale which largely surpasses the activity of his earthly ministry. As a consequence of the operation of the Spirit, which is due to the cross and resurrection, fellowship among human beings has become a reality, in a new and fruitful way, in the church, the body of Christ (e.g., Acts 2:42; 1 Cor 12). On the other hand, in Christ mankind has access to a communion with God (Eph 3:12). The plenitude of life implies the fullness of personal communion, with God in obedience and adoration, and with fellow-men in mutual service and common worship (Rev 7:9-12).

The unity of the cross and the resurrection.   In the intention of Jesus, as well as in the actual events of Calvary and Easter morning, the cross and resurrection form an indissoluble unity. From the point of view of human existence, true life could not have been achieved by other means than by taking the curse of death seriously and by overcoming it from within. Only so could death be made a gateway to life. That is a fundamental paradox, which, however, had been clearly divined and prefigured in the Old Testament. As has been pointed out, the formation of the resurrection faith in the early church is essentially due to a new understanding of Scripture (e.g., Lk 24:26 f.). And still this background does not cease to make most valuable contributions to a deeper understanding of the complexity of the ideas connected with salvation and life. In the light of Old Testament conceptions of worship, as well as in the experience of Christian worship from earliest times, the cross and the resurrection indicate a single and unique way to communion with God and men.

THE SACRAMENTS

From New Testament times Baptism and the Eucharist have occupied a predominant place in Christian worship. It is not as if they had been the only forms of worship or the most frequently used, but that in them the worship of the church is visualized more fully than in any other form, a fact which is evident already in the texts of the New Testament. All other forms of worship, common or private, are in some way dependent on the two central rites and receive their typically Christian sense and content from them. Thus, the use of the psalms and of certain prayers has been taken over from the synagogue, but when read in a Christian service, their wording becomes transparent in the light of the realities of Christian worship laid down in Baptism and the Eucharist. The life of every Christian, with regard to worship, has been inaugurated by the incorporation into the body of Christ. Continuously it derives, directly or indirectly, its vitality and inspiration from the Eucharist, which is in some way the pulse of the Christian community.

Institution by Christ of the sacraments. To a larger extent than was done some fifty years ago, scholars agree that the sacraments derive their origins from their institution by Christ. Being the central forms of Christian worship, they have not been created by human skill or by a human society. Therefore it is a decisive issue that the church is able to prove that Christ made the sacraments to be expressions of his redeeming work and to continue, during the time of the church in the period between pentecost and the parousia, the activity among men to which he devoted himself during his earthly ministry. In this respect recent exegetical research has made contributions to the comprehension of the imagery and symbolism underlying the biblical passages on the sacraments.

The sacraments and redemption. The sacraments mediate, within the living organism of the church, and to its members, the fruits of Christ's obedience and of his redeeming work. Thus Baptism is conceived as an incorporation into the death and the new life of Christ (Rom 6:3-5; cf. Col 2:12 f.; Eph 2:5-7). The decisive realities of human life, sin and death, are taken into full consideration and dealt with in the only thoroughly revolutionary way in order to establish new conditions and new relations. Therefore Baptism both actualizes and continues the work of Christ in giving human beings new possibilities of life and worship (Eph 2:5 f.).

In an analogous way the Eucharist continues to make Christians partakers of the life flowing forth from the cross and resurrection. Being taken into communion with him who served God by offering up his earthly life, and who now is the leader of heavenly worship, his followers are integrated into his worship and share in its life (1 Cor 10:16). If the hymn which introduces the epistle to the Colossians (1:15-20) can be considered to be a eucharistic prayer, the cosmic perspective of reconciliation enters directly into eucharistic practice and faith in the early church: "He has reconciled you in his body of flesh by his death, in order to present you holy and blameless and irreproachable before him" (v. 22), where the sacrificial terminology not only describes those who are saved by Christ as being his offering presented to God, but presupposes them to partake, in the presence of God, in the worship which the whole creation is bound to perform.

The incorporation of mankind into the redeemed life and the perfect worship of Christ cannot be accomplished apart from the personal faith of each individual concerned. This is a fact which is stressed by the writers of the apostolic age in connection with both Baptism (e.g., Rom 6:12 f.; Col 2:12) and the Eucharist (Col 1:23, "provided that you continue in the faith").

The symbolism which takes shape in the sacraments is plain and yet elaborate. The water of Baptism is—to mention only the main motifs—a sign of both purity (e.g., Eph 5:26; Heb 10:22) and life (e.g., Jn 3:5; 4:14; 7:38; Tit 3:5), evoking the atoning sacrifice of the cross and the perfect life of the resurrection (cf. Rev 22:1). This symbolism has its background in the ablutions of the temple cult and of Jewish practice, in proselyte baptism and in the rites of the Qumran. The bread and the wine of the Eucharist are symbols of the sacrifice and death of Christ, representing the breaking of his body, the outpouring of his blood, and the separation by death of the body and the blood. At the same time they are signs of the new life and of its fruits (cf. Rev 22:2), which are gifts of the risen Christ (cf. Jn 6:32-58, 2:1-10), and of the communion in his body (cf. Jn 15:1-8). Moreover, the Eucharist symbolizes the offering to God of human life and of its products, as well as the blessing of God which is given to all who serve him with their lives.

The unity of the cross and the resurrection in the sacraments. Both Baptism and the Eucharist are fruits of the redemptive work of Christ in its entirety. This is expressly stated in the fourth gospel. When Jesus having uttered the words "It is finished" (Jn 19:30) had died on the cross—and in the view of the fourth evangelist the cross is already the symbol of the exaltation of Christ (12:32)—blood and water came out of his side (19:34; cf. Heb 9:19; 1 Jn 5:6-8). In fact the sacraments are united not only by the common references to the death and resurrection of Christ but also by their roots in his ministry: the baptism in Jordan, the teaching on the baptism and cup of suffering (Mk 10:39), the meals with the disciples or with publicans and sinners, the feeding of the multitude, the Last Supper. At all these occasions—and there are still more of a similar kind— which prefigure different aspects of the sacraments, Jesus was acting as the son of man whose task it was to suffer and to die and then to rise again.

In the symbolism of its outward form Baptism unites the descent into death and the rise to a new life, a symbolism of which Jesus apparently was conscious when he stepped down into the water of the river Jordan to be baptized by John the Baptist. The motifs of descent and ascent, of cleansing and lifegiving water return simultaneously in the reflections on Baptism which are made in the writings of the early church. The whole of this symbolism clearly shows that the cross and the resurrection are equally underlying the sacramental theology of Baptism.

It is the same with the Eucharist. Its symbolism, too, is closely linked up with both the sacrifice of Calvary and the lifegiving event of Easter morning.

When the sacraments became signs and bearers of the redemptive work of Christ to human beings living in this world, they were also first-fruits of the new creation, pointing to the fullness of life which will be achieved on the last day, when the eschatological history of salvation reaches its final consummation. Thus the water of Baptism has its anti-type in the cosmic sea (Gen 1:2) and in the river of paradise (2:10 ff.), to which corresponds the eschatological river of the water of life (Rev 20:1). The Eucharist matches the

narrative of the loss of paradise and the words of God curs-
ing the ground (Gen 3:17-19). Bread and wine, being the
products of the earth and of human labor, became signs of
new possibilities of life and of blessing already in this world.
In a new, eschatological perspective the gift of God (through
Christ) and the worship of man meet in a realistic symbolism which expresses the fact of a new communion
between God and man, and between human beings in time
and the realm of the church.

The fourth gospel mentions neither the institution of Baptism nor of the Eucharist. This well-known fact is due to the
conviction of the evangelist that the exaltation of Christ on
the cross is the decisive act by which the sacraments in
reality were instituted (Jn 19:34). But also in the synoptic
gospels, as well as in the letters of the New Testament, the
sacraments center around the dying and rising of Christ.
Without the reality of the cross and the resurrection there
would be no real value in the sacraments. At the same time,
the lasting value of the redemptive acts of Christ is being
recalled and proclaimed continuously by the celebration of
Baptism and the Eucharist in the church.

THE LIFE OF THE CHURCH CONCEIVED AS WORSHIP

Just as the whole life of Christ can be considered to be worship in its purest and most consistent form, so the life of the
church is in its totality devoted to the worship of God
through Jesus Christ. The church gathers human beings
under new conditions which make it possible—as far as the
life of the new creation can be anticipated in this world—to
carry out, under the guidance of the Spirit, the original and
proper destiny of mankind: to serve and to worship God.
Therefore the church is concerned not only with forms of
worship in the narrow sense of the word, but with the totality
of human life in its relation to God. The function of the

church is expressed by two complexes of symbolical language which both occur in different layers in the writings of the New Testament, and therefore it can easily be seen that they seem to derive, in the final analysis, from the teaching of Jesus.

The new temple.   As has been demonstrated[1] it can reasonably be assumed that Jesus used the imagery of a new temple replacing that of Jerusalem in order to intimate the character of worship under new conditions resulting from his death and resurrection. What the Jewish cult and temple worship had aimed at would become a reality by means of his death and the creation of a spiritual body of his, the church (Mk 14:58 f.; Jn 2:21). Only when the true stone had been rejected and therefore paradoxically had become a corner-stone and a living stone (Mk 12:10; 1 Pet 2:4-8) would it become possible for human beings to be built, like living stones, into a spiritual house, an image which is to be interpreted not in a static but in a dynamic way (1 Pet 2:4; 1 Cor 3:10-17). It is obvious that not only in the interpretation of the early church (cf. the Shepherd of Hermas), but already in the intention of Jesus, the idea of a total worship was bound up with the necessity of the cross and the resurrection (cf. 2 Cor 5:1-5; Rev 21:22). True worship can be performed exclusively in the Spirit which is the result of Christ's saving work (Jn 4:23; cf. 1 Jn 5:7 f.).

The body of Christ.   An analogous symbolism, equally christological and closely related to that of the temple, is to be found in the concept of the body of Christ.[2] Though the imagery of the body has been elaborated mainly by St. Paul (e.g., 1 Cor 12; Eph 4 f.; Col 2 f.), its foundations seem to be contained in the symbolic action of the Last Supper: "This is my body" (Mk 14:22). And there again, the way

1. A. Cole, *The New Temple*, 1951.
2. J. A. T. Robinson, *The Body*, 1952.

to a living organism and an expanding communion goes through the breaking of the body ("which is for you," 1 Cor 11:24) and its resurrection. Because Christ had served his Father in his body, his followers, being incorporated into communion with him, become members of his spiritual body, which means that their bodies—being the outward form of their personality—are in the realm of life and can take part in the functions of true worship of God ("to present your bodies as a living sacrifice, holy and acceptable to God," Rom 12:1).

The unity of the cross and resurrection in the life of the church. As being a Christian means having been incorporated into the body of the risen Christ, one might think that the resurrection finally dominates the character of the church. But this is not so. As long as this age lasts, the church will bear also the marks of the cross. This implies that those who follow Christ must take up their cross in conformity with him (Mk 8:34). St. Paul speaks of Christ's afflictions which he has to complete in his flesh (Col 1:24), and he is well aware of the fact that suffering is a due part of a Christian's life (e.g., 1 Cor 4:10-13; 2 Cor 4:7-12; 6:4-10; 11:23-27; cf. 1 Pet 1:11). But simultaneously the new life, flowing forth from the victory of Christ, strengthens those who suffer. Therefore both cross and resurrection are present, as a matter of remembrance and continuous experience, in the worship of the church, in its prayers (e.g., Col 1:19-23) and its hymns (e.g., Phil 2:5-11; cf. Rev 5:11-13; 7:10). In consequence, the sacraments, as well as other forms of worship, will always have to be interpreted from Scripture in its entirety and confronted with the living experience of the church and all aspects of its life and functions. If one of the marks of Christian life definitely is martyrdom, that means that it profoundly differs from the natural life of this world. For the latter, when afflicted, goes to death, whereas the paradoxical way to the transcendent life goes through self-surrender, death and resurrection.

Anticipation of the fullness. There is a duality in Christian life, the necessity of suffering and the gift of the first-fruits of the Spirit. This duality reminds the church of the fact that the fullness of life cannot be reached in this world, but can yet give a new character to life in this age. There are, within the church, possibilities of anticipation of the final perfection. The church, together with all creation, waits with eager longing for the accomplishment of God's mysteries, his plan of salvation. In its worship, the church realizes that the cross and resurrection are not only events in history, but remain to be the foundations of Christian hope, warrants of the final salvation and of the godly life of the age to come. Christ who will reveal himself in final glory on the day of his parousia, is living and reigning now, and will return as the one who suffered and died and rose again as the prince of life (1 Thess 4:14; 2 Thess 1:7-10).

ATONEMENT AND LIFE IN HEAVENLY WORSHIP

In the worship of the church not only the coherence of the cross and resurrection, but the profound unity of the redemptive work of Christ and of its forthcoming consummation become evident. What is characteristic of the interpretation of the person and work of Christ, which is given in the different writings of the New Testament, is that they were not only temporary means to counteract and to overcome the disastrous consequences of the fall, but that they have an eternal value, which means that they are everlasting testimonies of the obedient worship of Christ and of the love of God.

This theme has been worked out particularly in the epistle to the Hebrews and in the book of Revelation. Having made atonement once for all in order to sanctify mankind (Heb

10:10), Christ sat down at the right hand of God as an eternal high priest (vv. 12, 21).[3] He will remain the mediator of the new covenant (Heb 9:15).

Similarly, in the visions of John the apostle, Christ, when he stands in the heavenly congregation and in front of the throne of God, is still the lamb as it had been slain (Rev 5:6; cf. 7:9; 14:1). Though exalted into heaven, Christ remains the one who had sacrificed himself to redeem mankind. In the imagery of the final consummation (Rev 21 f.), the lamb is the bridegroom of the people of God (21:9), and likewise the lamb, that is the Christ of Calvary, is together with God almighty "the temple" (21:22; 22:3), and this means that he is both subject and object of the true and eternal worship.

Thus, the heavenly Christ is and will always be the Christ of the cross and the resurrection. So he has become and will remain the source of life of the new creation and of the eternal people of God. He unites them in the worship of the new temple, and he makes them partakers of his life and therefore members of his body. But participation in heavenly worship and eternal life must not be thought of as a static wearing of white robes and holding of palm branches (Rev 7:9). The symbolism of the river of life and the tree of life, as well as of the city of God (Rev 22:1 ff.) intimate a variety of social life, the characteristic feature of which is the freedom from limitation and destruction by sin and death. A social gospel for the world of today will always have to make clear that improvements of the conditions of human life can be made only as far as they are anticipations of the transcendent life.

Finally one can ask whether there is a difference between the life of the first couple of human beings in the garden of

---

3. Cf. W. Hahn, *Gottesdienst und Opfer Christi,* 1951.

Eden and the life of the eschatological community in the age to come. The answer will be affirmative: there is a fundamental difference, and it lies precisely in the cross and the resurrection. The life coming forth from the resurrection can, because of the perfect sacrifice and atonement of the cross, never be exposed to another disastrous temptation and fall.

Thus humanity and the whole creation is released from the desolate expectation which is characteristic of Indian religion and which was not foreign either to the Graeco-Roman world of the period of the early church: the wheel of time brings about the ages in a never-ceasing recapitulation. The cross and the resurrection are warrants of a final fullness of life, the meaning of which is divine worship and is revealed in the worship of the church.

Come, Creator Spirit! For the Renewal of Worship and Witness

THOMAS F. TORRANCE

What do we mean by the prayer, *Come, Creator Spirit?* It cannot mean that the Holy Spirit should come and act as in the original creation of the world or in its creative preservation, and yet it is a prayer for his creative power. It is a prayer for the Holy Spirit in accordance with his new coming and acting as on the day of Pentecost. On that day the Holy Spirit came into the world and entered into the experience of men in a way that had never happened before. Certainly the Spirit continued to operate in the world and to be at work among men as he had been from the beginning, but at Pentecost something quite new happened, as new and distinct, and indeed as unique, as the incarnation itself. Along with the birth, life, death, resurrection and ascension of Christ, the pouring out of his Spirit at Pentecost belongs to the series of God's mighty acts which brought salvation to mankind and inaugurated the new age. They are acts which cannot be repeated and cannot be undone, for they have entirely altered the relation of the world to God. From that point all history presses relentlessly forward to its consummation when Christ will come again to judge the quick and the dead and make all things new. We live on this side of Pentecost and are on our way to meet the Advent Christ. We live, therefore, after the new thing has happened, within the new age in which the Creator Spirit of God is abroad among men and actively at work among them in a new and distinctive way, in addition to his original and continuing operation in the world. *Come, Creator Spirit* is a prayer of participation in this new happening, a prayer in which we allow it to overtake us; it is a prayer in which we ask that the new mode of the Spirit's entry into the lives of men at Pentecost may not be obstructed in our own experience.

How, then, are we to understand this distinctively new mode of the Holy Spirit's activity in the experience of men?

It is in the *incarnation* and the *atonement* that we learn the secret of Pentecost. With the incarnation, God the eternal Son became man, without ceasing to be God and without breaking the communion of the holy Trinity within which God lives his own divine life. Jesus became the bearer of the Holy Spirit among men. Because Jesus made our flesh of sin his very own and wrought out in himself peace and reconciliation between man and God, he became not only the bearer but the mediator of the Holy Spirit to men.

Now we may understand the distinctively new mode of the Spirit's coming into the experience of men. The inner life of the holy Trinity is extended to include human nature in and through Jesus. This is the way that the divine love has taken to redeem man, by making him share in the holy power in which God lives his own divine life. The pouring out of that power from on high took place at Pentecost, with the entry of the Holy Spirit in his new mode of presence and activity into the experience of mortal men. On our lips the prayer, *Come, Creator Spirit,* is a prayer of commitment to what God has already done in Jesus Christ, and a prayer of participation in the divine nature, in the faith that it is only the power of God which can redeem fallen man, and that nothing short of the very life and breath of God himself can renew the life of his people. Hence for the church to worship God is to draw into itself the holy breath of the life of God, and to live out that divine life on earth is to live a life of praise and witness to his glory.

That is the church's belief in the Holy Spirit which it confesses in the Nicene Creed. "And I believe in the Holy Spirit, the Lord and Giver of Life, who proceeds from the Father and the Son, who with the Father and the Son together is worshiped and glorified, who spoke by the prophets." It is in the Nicene (Constantinopolitan) Creed, which is essentially a doxological act in which worship and witness combine inseparably together, that the church's faith in the Holy Spirit first came into clear articulation. By his very nature the Holy Spirit not only proceeds from the Father but lifts up to the Father. He is not only the Spirit sent by Christ but the Spirit of response to Christ, the Spirit in whom and by whom and with whom we worship and glorify the Father and the Son. Not only is he God the Holy Spirit descending to us, the Spirit by whom God bears witness to himself, but God the Holy Spirit lifting up all creation in praise and rejoicing in God, himself the Spirit of worship and witness, by whom the church lives and fulfills its mission to the glory of God.

THE NEW COMING OF THE HOLY SPIRIT AT PENTECOST WAS A COMING IN THE UTTER GODNESS OF GOD

We have become accustomed to think of the coming of the Holy Spirit far too much as the interiorizing in our hearts of divine salvation, with the result that the presence of the Spirit is so often identified with inward moral and religious states. Creator Spirit and our own creative spirituality tend to become confused. Certainly the Holy Spirit is sent into our hearts where he begets enlightenment and conviction, and bears witness with our spirit that we are the children of God, but the psychologizing and subjectivizing of this is entirely, or almost entirely, absent from the New Testament. The emphasis of the apostolic church was placed elsewhere. Pentecost meant the living presence of God among men in all his transcendent power and holiness. The emphasis is not upon man receiving but upon God giving, for man receives only as he falls under the transcendent power of the Creator Spirit, who gives himself to man even when he has no power to receive, so that man's reception of the Holy Spirit is itself a creative work of God.

Let me plead for a reconsideration by the Reformed Churches of what the Greek Fathers called *theosis*. This is usually, but unfortunately, translated *deification*. But it has no more to do with the *divinization* of man than the incarnation has to do with the humanization of God. *Theosis* was the term the Fathers used to emphasize the fact that through the Spirit we have to do with God in his utter sublimity, his sheer Godness or holiness; creatures though we are, men on earth, in the Spirit we are made to participate in saving acts that are abruptly and absolutely divine—election, adoption, regeneration or sanctification—and we participate in them by grace alone. *Theosis* describes man's involvement in such a mighty act of God upon him that he is raised up to find the true center of his existence not in himself but in holy God, where he lives and moves and has his being in the uncreated but creative energy of the Holy Spirit. By *theosis* the Greek Fathers wished to express the fact that in the new coming of the Holy Spirit we are up against *God* in the most absolute sense, God in his ultimate holiness or Godness.

Man in the weakness and lowliness of creaturely human being is by God made free for God through the power of the Creator Spirit, who is not and will not be limited in his acts by man's weakness or creaturehood or his lack of capacity. *Theosis* is an attempt to express the staggering significance of Pentecost as the coming from on high, from outside of us and beyond us, of divine power. Is there anything we need to regain more than this faith in the utter Godness of God the Holy Spirit?

IN HIS NEW COMING THE HOLY SPIRIT IS MEDIATED BY CHRIST AND AT THE SAME TIME MEDIATES CHRIST TO US

It is in grasping the mutual relation between the work of Christ and the work of the Spirit that we may understand what worship and its renewal really mean.

(1) In his new coming the Holy Spirit is mediated to us through Christ in his divine and human natures. As God he gave his Spirit to men, for only God can give God. As man he received the Spirit of God in our human nature and mediated it to his brethren through himself. Jesus Christ was never without the Spirit, for as the eternal Son he ever remained in the unity of the Spirit and of the Father, but as the incarnate Son on earth he was given the Spirit without measure and consecrated in his human nature for his mission as the vicarious servant. He came through the temptations in the wilderness clothed with the power of the Spirit and went forth to bring in the kingdom of God by meeting and defeating the powers of darkness entrenched in human flesh. He struggled and prayed in the Spirit with unspeakable cries of agony, and bore in his Spirit the full burden of human evil and woe. Through the eternal Spirit he offered himself without spot to the Father in sacrifice for sin; according to the Spirit of holiness he was raised from the dead, and ascended to the right hand of the Father to receive all power in heaven and earth. There he attained the ground from which he could pour out the Spirit of God upon all flesh. As lamb of God and priest of our human nature, he sent down from the throne of the most high the gift of the Holy Spirit upon his church, that through the same Spirit the Father and the Son might dwell with men.

Jesus Christ, true God and true man, is thus the mediator of the Holy Spirit, being himself both the God who gives and the man who receives in one person. In his new coming, therefore, the Spirit came as the Spirit of Jesus. He came as the Spirit who in Jesus has penetrated into a new intimacy with our human nature, for he came as the Spirit in whom Jesus lived through our human life from birth to death, and beyond into the resurrection. It is still in the name of Jesus Christ that the Holy Spirit comes to us, and in no other name.

(2) The Holy Spirit is mediated to us only through the glorification of Christ. Jesus Christ was himself the bearer in our human nature of the fullness of the Spirit, but the Spirit in his new mode of presence and activity could not be transmitted to others when they were yet in their sins, or be received by others until atonement for sin was completed and the mediator took his place on the throne of God in his consecrated and glorified humanity. Only with the taking up of the glorified humanity of Christ our brother into the unity of the blessed Trinity, could the Holy Spirit be released in all his sanctifying and renewing agency to dwell with man. Then he came down freely upon the body that had been prepared, the church purchased by the blood of Christ, and lifted it up, unhindered by guilt and sin or the divine judgment, to participate freely in the very life of God.

There is one mediator between God and man, the man Christ Jesus. The Holy Spirit comes to us only through him as the Spirit of holiness, the Spirit of redemption, and the Spirit of glory. He comes to us from the inner life of Jesus, and therefore he comes as the Spirit of a manhood wholly offered to God in perpetual glorification, worship, praise.

What do we learn from this about the renewal of the Church's worship?

The Holy Spirit is God in his freedom, not only to give

being to creation, but, through his presence to it, to bring its relations with himself to their end and perfection. He is the Spirit who goes forth from God and returns to God. This answers to the two-fold work of the Son when he came down for us and for our salvation and was made man, and when he ascended again to the Father, presenting to him the humanity which he had sanctified and redeemed in the atoning oblation of himself. It is the same two-fold work which took place at Pentecost in the manward and in the Godward movement of the Holy Spirit, supervening upon the church and lifting it upward in its faith and rejoicing in God.

It is through the power of the Spirit who came down at Pentecost that we are united to Christ in his identification with us and in his self-consecration and self-offering for us. We have no other answer to the will of God, no other offering, no other response or worship, for without Christ we can do nothing. The Spirit which Christ breathes upon us, then, becomes the Spirit of our response to him and through him to the Father. Thus in our worship the Holy Spirit comes forth from God, uniting us to the response and obedience and faith and prayer of Jesus, and returns to God, raising us up in Jesus to participate in the worship of heaven and in the eternal communion of the holy Trinity.

If the Holy Spirit is himself the immediate agent of our worship, he is also the immediate agent of its renewal. He realizes in us the re-creative power of the risen and glorified humanity of Christ. Now it cannot be emphasized sufficiently that it is through atonement that we are renewed, through the obedience of the holy one in our flesh and through the blood of Christ shed for us; and that it is only after the completion of Christ's sacrifice for sin, his self-presentation before the Father and the pouring out of the Holy Spirit upon us, that the atonement became effective for the remission of our sins and the cleansing of our conscience. From beginning to end it is through the *holiness* of Jesus that we are redeemed and regenerated. Therefore when the Holy Spirit comes to us as the agent of our renewal, he comes not only as the Holy Spirit of the one eternal God but as the Spirit mediated through Christ Jesus and charged with his divine-human holiness. He renews us by drawing us within the self-consecration of Christ made on our behalf and by assimilating us into his holiness. The Holy Spirit renews only through sanctification. If Jesus himself was raised from the dead according to the Spirit of holiness, it cannot be otherwise with us.

It cannot be otherwise with our worship: renewal may come only through sanctification. Conformity to the holiness and humanity of Jesus Christ is the test that must be applied to all our forms of worship. Are they really expressions of the holy mind and will of God incarnate in Jesus, or are they after all but forms of our own self-expression? Is our worship a constant participation in the holiness of Christ, in his own inner victory over sin and temptation, in his perfect oneness in mind and will with God? Is it the lifting up of our hearts through the Son in the Spirit to the Father? Is it a holding up of Christ in his finished work before heaven as our only offering and prayer? Or is it the manifestation of our own piety adapted to the pattern of this present world in forms of our own choosing? Have we not obtruded upon God will-worship of our own, which in the last analysis is little more than the worship of self or the holding up of our own spirituality? And is not the deepest reason for this that we have lost touch with the Spirit of holiness? Surely degeneration in worship springs from a weakening in our sense of the utter holiness and majesty of the most high and an estrangement from the creative source of holiness among men, the sanctified and sanctifying humanity of Jesus.

IN HIS NEW COMING THE HOLY SPIRIT FOCUSES ATTENTION
UPON JESUS CHRIST, AND ENABLES US TO BELIEVE IN HIM
AND BEAR FAITHFUL WITNESS TO HIM AS SAVIOR OF THE
WORLD

If the vicarious life and mediatorial work of Christ led to
the supreme gift of the Holy Spirit, the function of the Spirit
was not to bear witness to himself but to bear witness to
Christ as God and savior, and through his glorification to
gather all who believe in him into the unity and communion
of Father, Son and Holy Spirit.

The Holy Spirit is not knowable independently in himself,
but he is known through the one Word or self-revelation of
God in Jesus Christ. We know who he is because he creates
in us beyond all creaturely or human capacities the ability
to know the unknowable, and therein reveals himself as
Creator Spirit of the living God. The Spirit does not utter
himself but utters the Word. He does not incarnate himself
but incarnates the Son. He does not show his own face, but
shows us the Father in the face of the Son. Yet as he comes
to us from the Father and from the Son, he confronts us in
himself with all the ultimate Godness of the Godhead, before
whom we can only bow in worship and adoration, and with
all the reverence and obedience of our minds. We know him
as no less Lord God, the Creator, than the Father and the
Son, for he is the limitless power of all creation and re-creation, God the Holy Spirit in all the freedom and majesty of
the eternal being.

Such is the Spirit who bears witness to Christ, for Christ
is not known and believed on the ground of human testimony but only on the ground of testimony that comes from
God himself. So long as Holy Spirit was not yet abroad
among men, even the disciples were dull of hearing and slow
in their understanding, and could not grasp the bewildering

miracle of Jesus, for they stumbled and groped like men blinded by light. The Spirit was not yet because Christ was not yet glorified, for until the consummation of atonement the Holy Spirit could not come upon them and they could not receive him without being consumed.

But the promise of the Paraclete was given: the Spirit of truth would be sent to them and then they would know.

And the promise was fulfilled, in the gift of the Holy Spirit. When the Spirit came upon them they received power, for the Spirit both testified to them of Christ, creating in them understanding and faith, and made them witnesses themselves to Christ before the world, creating in them the sphere where Christ continues to be heard and to be believed. Thus through the coming of the Spirit, God brings his self-revelation to its fulfillment, for the Spirit is the creative subject of God's revelation to us and the creative subject in our reception and understanding of that revelation. The Holy Spirit does not do this by continuing a work begun by Christ and now left off by him, as if we now passed from the economy of the Son into the economy of the Spirit. On the contrary, through the Spirit, in and with his coming, Christ himself returns to be present among us, living and speaking and operating in the church which, through the Spirit, is constituted his body on earth and in history. The presence of the Holy Spirit in the church means that it is the living Lord himself who is here in his redeeming and sanctifying activity. The office of the Holy Spirit in the church is not to call attention to himself apart from Christ, but to focus all attention on Christ, to glorify him, to bear witness to his deity, to testify to his mind and will, and in him and through him to lead us to the Father. He is God the Spirit by whom we know God, for he is God the Spirit by whom God bears witness to himself. Transparence and self-effacement thus belong to the very nature and office of the Holy Spirit, as the Spirit of the Father and the Spirit of the Son.

On earth there is no kingdom of the Spirit, and no body of the Spirit, but only a kingdom of Christ and a body of Christ through the Spirit, for the Spirit is present and at work among us in his transparent and self-effacing nature. It is his office constantly to call the church out of the world and to create it as the sphere within which he realizes and perpetuates among men God's own witness to himself. In the church, as we have seen, the Holy Spirit exercises a Godward ministry as he acts from the side of men, uplifting their worship in Christ to the heavenly Father. But in the church he also exercises that Godward ministry in that he creates and empowers from the side of men a witness to Christ as God and Savior of mankind, and so constitutes the corporate witness of the whole church as the mode of God's own witness to himself among men. This does not mean that the church now takes the place of Christ in his absence, continuing or extending the work which he began, but that the church is chosen to be the locus of his presence among men and that he himself, the risen Lord, is at work in and through it, yet transcending it in the freedom and power of his Spirit. For in spite of the constant failure and inadequacy of the church, Christ fulfills through it his one ministry as prophet, priest and king, on earth as in heaven.

In order to see the bearing of this upon the renewal of the church's witness, we must consider further the *creativity* and the *transparency* of the Holy Spirit, for in his regenerative and recreative work the Holy Spirit remains the free creative agent of all God's ways and works, and the uncreated transparent light of his self-revelation.

With the coming of the Holy Spirit at Pentecost God's redemptive and creative acts merged together. It was a movement of recreation through atoning sanctification, for through the *Holy* Spirit the full creative impact of the divine word broke in upon the apostolic church, constituting it a new creation in Christ, fulfilling in it the sanctifying and regenerating of our human nature that had already taken place in Christ, and so bringing it into a new state of being in which it was renewed after the image of God. The Holy Spirit was the quickening breath of this new creation, breathed out by God upon the church and breathed in by the church as it came to life under his power. He was the Spirit speaking the word of God to the church and creating within it faithful hearing and understanding of the word, the Spirit testifying to the mighty acts of God in Christ and the Spirit of response to Christ in the church forming it unto the obedience of faith in him. Not only did he act creatively upon the church in the giving of life and the distributing of his manifold gifts, but he brought his creative work to its completion or end in the establishment of the church as the body of Christ, the new sphere of existence in him. He was the Creator Spirit acting always both from the side of God toward man and from the side of man toward God.

What does it mean for us to come up against the *creative* activity of the Spirit in this way? What does it mean for our witness in the church that the *Creator* Spirit should dwell with fallen man and recreate him in his knowledge and understanding of God? Fallen man is described in the Scriptures as man attempting to emancipate himself from the Creator, man snatching the very freedom God has given him in order to make himself and reproduce his own image, and therefore as man who even imposes the images of his own devising and fashioning upon God. In this way he changes the truth of God into a lie and worships and serves the creature more than the Creator, for he changes the glory of the uncorruptible God into an image made like to corruptible man. That is to say, man carries the sin whereby he fell into his continuing relations with God, and substitutes his own creativity for that of the Creator Spirit even in the realm of the knowledge and worship of God. Indeed, it is in religion that man is most tempted to do this, so that religious forms can become the supreme expression of his sin.

Now the coming of the Creator Spirit as at Pentecost is the point where man's own sinful creativity has to be broken, where man in his Adamic existence, man as he created himself, must be stripped of his own image and come to an end. For in the coming of the Spirit fallen man is brought up against the final power of the Creator himself. At that point he is either re-created and emancipated from himself for genuine faith in God, or he lapses back, in conflict with the Spirit, into his own self-willed existence and becomes even more securely imprisoned within his own inventions. Then the light that is in him is darkness indeed.

Is that not the story of those recalcitrant Israelites who, out of their own distinctive piety and attitude to existence, had forged their own conception of the messiah. They even bent the oracles and ordinances of grace to serve their end, and projected their own man-made traditions upon the word of God, making it of no effect. And so they strove to become masters of their own destiny. Then when at last the messiah actually came, the conflict between their own image of God and that mediated by the messiah was so intense that instead of surrendering to the creative impact of his Spirit upon them, they crucified the messiah, and in a desperate attempt to force the hand of God they even resisted his Holy Spirit. Was that not the verdict of the martyr Stephen? "Ye do always resist the Holy Spirit: as your fathers did, so do you." And they stoned him to death.

Must we not ask whether this is not also the story of the Christian Church, even in modern times? Have we not also been at work forging our own image of God out of our own vaunted prior understanding, or out of the depth of our own being, out of our own existential decisions and our own creative spirituality? Have we not also constructed our own

conceptions of Christ to suit our self-willed attitude to existence in the twentieth century? And then have we not been
trying to justify ourselves by projecting this way of thinking
back upon the apostolic church, alleging that its image of
Christ is little more than the product of its own creative
spirituality or the expression of its attitude to existence? And
so have we not been busy crucifying again the Christ of the
apostolic witness and resisting the Creator Spirit of Pentecost, substituting the creativity of men in place of the holy
creativity of God?

The supreme questions must be asked once again. Do we
really believe in the Holy Spirit? Do we believe that at Pentecost he came upon the apostolic witnesses as the Creator
Spirit and, in spite of the distorting preconceptions of the
human heart and the creative projections of the human
spirit, transformed their understanding to receive God's own
witness to himself in Jesus Christ, and so empowered them
to become faithful witnesses to Christ themselves? Do we
believe the *kerygma* of Jesus Christ to be the creation of
God's Spirit, or the creation of man's own religious consciousness? In short, do we really believe in Jesus Christ as
God and Savior?

Surely the New Testament makes it abundantly clear that
the Holy Spirit is given to those who believe in Jesus and
that we grow in the grace and knowledge of Christ as we
surrender to the creative impact of the Holy Spirit upon us,
but that unbelief grieves the presence of the Spirit and
quenches his power among us. What else is unbelief but
resistance to the Holy Spirit, and what can obstruct the
renewal of the church and destroy its witness more than
unbelief? Let it be said quite bluntly that what we need
urgently is a renewal of faith: of belief in Jesus Christ as in
reality God himself incarnate among men, of belief in the
cross as the objective intervention of God in human exist-

ence for the salvation of mankind, and of belief in the resurrection of Jesus Christ from the dead in body as the first-fruits of the new creation. The renewal of our witness will only come as we surrender ourselves to the miraculous divine power of the Creator Spirit, and commit ourselves to faith in Jesus Christ as God and Savior.

Now if this faith is to be strong and our witness is to be clear, we must guard against the impurities that arise when we seek to perfect the operation of the Spirit by our own works and so obtrude ourselves into the evangelical message. This is where the transparency of the Spirit comes in, for to be genuine our witness must be shot through and through with the uncreated light of God's self-revelation. Then alone can it be the means of God's own witness to himself among men.

In all our knowledge and proclamation of God in worship and witness, we make use of human and earthly forms of thought and speech, cognitive, linguistic or liturgical forms, but in themselves these forms are quite opaque as far as their reference to God himself is concerned. In themselves they are merely expressions of human and earthly activity, and reveal not God but man. If they are really to serve their purpose they must be made to point beyond themselves to the divine realities they are meant to signify. That can happen only through the power of the Holy Spirit as he himself testifies of God in and through them, for he alone can make the forms of faith and witness transparent by making the reality of God shine through them. Only through the sanctifying presence of the Holy Spirit emancipating us from ourselves is Jesus Christ, the incarnate Word, allowed to sound through to us and to take control of our proclamation, and therefore to confront men directly and personally through our witness.

Consider, for example, the sacrament of Baptism. The

meaning of Baptism does not lie in the external rite or simply its performance, but solely in Jesus Christ himself, for Baptism directs us and our children to the saving act of God's love which he has already fulfilled for us in Jesus Christ. Therefore we interpret Baptism not by looking at what we do, but by looking through the rite to Christ and his Gospel and by allowing Christ and his Gospel through the power of the Spirit to break through to us. Without sacramental transparence Baptism becomes blind and meaningless.

If it is only through that kind of transparency that the divine ordinance of Baptism is an effective means of God's own self-witness, how desperately do we stand in need of the same transparence in the renewal of our witness?

Let us recall that this transparence comes from the Holy Spirit, from his own self-effacing nature and office. But if we turn our attention to the Spirit independently instead of turning our attention with the Spirit to Christ, or try to make the Spirit visible through perfecting his operation by our own works, then we violate the holiness of the Spirit by resisting him in his self-effacing office and confusing him with our own spirits. Thus everything becomes opaque, for we fail to distinguish him in whom we believe from our own believing, and in our proclamation we confound the earthen vessel with the heavenly treasure. We mix up ourselves with Christ and so darken witness and obscure vision of the savior.

Renewal of witness will come surely through the holiness of Jesus and renewal of our worship in him, that is, through the sanctifying and recreating power of the Holy Spirit lifting us again out of ourselves in Christ to worship the Father. Only the Spirit of holiness can purge us from the falsification of the Good News brought about by mixing up with it our own subjectivities and unrealities. Only the Creator Spirit begetting in us the simplicity of faith can make us free from ourselves and the distortion in our understanding of the Gospel through our own preconceptions and inventions. Yet it is against the Holy Spirit that we have sinned, in substituting our own creativity for his, and in resisting his truth in the apostolic witness. Therefore we need to be cleansed anew by the blood of Christ and receive afresh the Spirit he mediates to us through his atonement. Without the transparence of the Spirit we cannot exercise the kind of witness in which God in Christ bears witness to himself. It is only when God's own self-witness is heard that the world will believe.

Worship and the Ascension of Christ

BORIS BOBRINSKOY

Before studying the mystery of Christ's ascension and of his heavenly priesthood, as projected in the liturgy, we will devote an introductory section to their setting in the New Testament and in the tradition of the early church. We shall then show how the liturgical service is a sacramental participation in these mysteries.

IN THE NEW TESTAMENT AND THE TRADITION OF THE EARLY CHURCH

A real analysis of the facts described in the New Testament would lead us too far from our subject and beyond our competence. But one thing must be pointed out: the church made a clear choice between the various narratives and descriptions of Christ's ascension which were known in the middle of the second century, and it firmly excluded from the canon the apocryphal stories which described so naively and so boldly the actual way in which Christ ascended into heaven, to the amazement of the angelic hierarchies. Amid the extremely divergent descriptions of the ascension, and through the multiplicity of detail, the church has retained in the Bible only the *terrestrial* and the *transcendent* aspects of the mystery of the ascension. The terrestrial aspect is given through the statement of the apostles who were eye-witnesses of the ascension, humbly relating their tangible experience of Christ's disappearance and their return to Jerusalem "in

great joy" (Lk 24:52). It is the paradoxical joy of separation, a real joy due to the certainty of the coming of "the
other Comforter" promised to them by Jesus (Lk 24:49;
Jn 17:7), and through whom he will himself be present in
the world. The transcendent aspect of the mystery, which
is the only aspect important for faith, is "the ascension of the
risen Christ to the divine world of glory. Christ's invisible,
transcendent accession to the divine world is clearly the
essential part of the mystery. His visible departure from this
world is only a secondary aspect of it. This explains why
early Christian tradition laid so much stress upon the essential affirmation of Christ's triumph in heaven."[1]

The description of the ascension is found in many sources
in the tradition of the early church, both in the apocryphal

---

1. P. Benoit, "L'Ascension," *Revue Biblique,* 5 (1949), p. 195. It is
scarcely necessary to insist on the fact that according to the testimony of
the evangelists Christ's ascension to the right hand of the Father has two
things to teach us: a) *that which concerns his elevation into the glory of
the Father.* The right hand of the Father must not be thought of as meaning a particular place or location but rather in the sense of the glory and
honor which the incarnate Word had before the creation of the world,
and which returns to him once more. Christ's exaltation is a qualificative
concept and demonstrates the distinction and the substantial distance
between the Creator and the creature, the eternal and the temporal: it
implies no less the unbreakable link—the bridge *(pontifex)* between these
two opposite concepts. Christ united with glorified human nature is raised
to the bosom of the Father. This mystery, incomprehensible to natural
reason, is the basis of the dogma of the ascension. b) The second teaching
of the New Testament is *that which concerns the presence of Christ in
the world* (Mt 28:20). This presence is made effective by the action of
the Holy Spirit who witnesses to Christ, who is the Spirit of Christ, who
perpetuates Christ in the church by means of the sacramental life, who
incorporates us into Christ. This double presence of Christ at the right
hand of the Father and in the world does not imply a contradiction:
rather does it resolve it into an "antimony," for Christ's presence in the
Holy Spirit is nothing other than our elevation following upon his into
the glory and the intimacy of the Father.
Father Serge Boulgakoff has brought out very clearly this double
aspect—terrestrial and celestial—of the ascension and high priesthood of
Christ in "l'Agneau Divin" (a chapter on the priesthood of Christ and
the ascension in *Du Verbe Incarné,* French translation: Paris, Aubier,
1943).

writings (the Ascension of Isaiah, the Epistles of the Apostles, the Apocalypse of Peter) and in the writings of the Fathers and teachers of the church (Justin, Hermas, Irenaeus, Origen, Athanasius, Gregory of Nazianzus, Gregory of Nyssa, Chrysostom, Ambrose, John of Damascus, Gregory Palamas).

Usually the Fathers reproduce not only the narrative of the evangelists but also the facts of the apocryphal writings relating to Christ's ascension into heaven, at the stupefaction and admiration of the angelic powers in face of the triumph of the Savior physically entering heaven, and sitting in our human form upon the very throne of God. That is the main theme of the festival of the Ascension, which is the liturgical expression of this same primitive tradition. The essential truth taught us here by the church is that Christ's ascension is not only an event in his earthly life, but a drama played out in the sphere of the spiritual creation, and that it is in the spiritual sphere that it receives its true cosmic proportion.

In the progressive elaboration of the theme of the ascension, certain messianic psalms have played an outstanding part. For instance Psalm 24:7-10 (a dialogue between the angels and their stupefaction when Christ glorified enters into heaven; this theme is not found in the New Testament, but apocryphal writings and the Fathers of the church frequently apply it to the mystery of the ascension); Psalm 68:18 (exaltation of the messiah who has ascended on high and liberated the captives; this psalm is quoted in connection with the ascension in Ephesians 4:7-9); and finally Psalm 110:1-4 where the messiah-king is seated at the right hand of God and is victorious over his enemies (1 Cor 15:25-26; Rom 8:34, and Heb 10:12-13; in the Creed of Nicaea-Constantinople, and in the writings of the early Fathers).

Although the ascension of Christ and his session on the right hand of the Father are attested by the writers of the

New Testament, and in the early church, the festival of the Ascension does not appear as such until the fourth century—first in the church at Jerusalem which desired to recall the mysteries of our redemption at the place and on the actual anniversary of the day when they occurred. The celebration of the ascension very soon spread to all the churches within Christendom. From the fourth century onwards, therefore, we find sermons preached on Ascension Day (Gregory of Nyssa, John Chrysostom). Probably the pre-Nicaean church celebrated the Ascension at Pentecost; and the whole of Eastertide (50 days) was probably devoted to the common and indivisible celebration of the glorious mysteries of Christ, without special emphasis on the ascension, but in general meditation upon the exaltation of our Savior in the resurrection and ascension.

THE HEAVENLY DIMENSION OF REDEMPTION IN THE EPISTLE TO THE HEBREWS[2]

More than any other book of the New Testament, the epistle to the Hebrews, together with the book of Revelation, reveals the heavenly aspect of the sacrifice of the lamb. It

---

2. A question which it is legitimate to ask here is whether the conception of sacrifice which the epistle to the Hebrews develops fully corresponds to the redemptive work accomplished by Christ: in other words, whether the sacrificial terminology of the epistle to the Hebrews has not been applied in too systematic and arbitrary a manner to the eucharistic liturgy in early tradition. In this age-long controversy between reformed and "catholic" theologians on the problem of the sacrificial character of the Eucharist I would particularly like to mention from the Protestant side the recent book by Max Thurian, *The Eucharistic Memorial* (Richmond, 1961). The author is here attempting to give value once more to the idea of liturgical sacrifice. Father Spicq has abundantly demonstrated the New Testament affinities of the epistle to the Hebrews: cf. "L'origine johannique de la conception du Christ-prêtre dans l'épître aux Hebreux" in *Aux Sources de la tradition chrétienne* (Neuchâtel and Paris, 1959), pp. 258-269; *L'Epître aux Hebreux, I. Introduction* (Paris, 1952), pp. 109-168. Cf. Congar, *The Mystery of the Temple* (Westminster, 1962), p. 170.

shows the messiah's work of redemption to be essentially sacrificial. Through the Son's voluntary self-sacrifice, mankind is reconciled with the Father who accepts the oblation. Saint Paul expresses this idea in a passage which is of direct concern for the ascension: "Christ being come a high priest of good things to come . . . by his own blood entered in once into the holy place, having obtained eternal redemption for us" (Heb 9:11; cf. 4:14; 8:1; 9:24; 10:12-23; 12:2). The holy of holies, the heavenly sanctuary, is the glorious presence of the Father, of which the temple at Jerusalem was the figure, the altars within our churches being the sacramental representation of that holy sacrifice.[3] The priesthood exercised by Jesus during his earthly life is eternal; it is carried out in the heavenly sanctuary. It is in heaven that the sacrifice of the cross is accepted, before the hidden altar of God's glory. Since his ascension, Jesus has been enthroned at the right hand of God. He has penetrated into the heavenly sanctuary, and God's promise has been fulfilled, "Thou art a priest for ever after the order of Melchizedek." The eternal priesthood in accordance with the order of Melchizedek is carried on in the presence of the Father. "For Christ is not entered into the holy places made with hands, which are the figures of the true; but into heaven itself, now to appear in the presence of God for us" (Heb 9:24), and from there he intercedes as a mediator for mankind, and dispenses the good things to come (Heb 9:11).

It is from the two-fold perspective—both earthly and

3. Father Congar has devoted his book *The Mystery of the Temple* to the study of the presence of God in the Old and New Testament. He shows authoritatively how the temple and the sacrifices of the old covenant are replaced by the very person of Christ, whose body is the true sanctuary of God and how this presence is continued in the church as the temple of God and in the Christian as the temple of the Holy Spirit, and finally how this presence is realized in the terrestrial dimension and also eschatologically in heaven in the last days.

heavenly—of the mystery of our redemption as described in Hebrews, that we are able to understand the work of the risen Christ in connection with his sacrifice. The suffering and glory of Christ at Easter, his resurrection from the dead, his ascension into heaven and his enthronement at the right hand of the Father have been accomplished in history, in "the last days" once for all, so that they have a universal range and a cosmic scope. But we must not lose sight of the heavenly, supra-historic dimension of the mystery of our salvation which includes and gathers together the "time" of divine foreknowledge (1 Pet 1:20; Rev 13:8; 17:8), the time of the preparation and of the prophetic visions, the time of realization in history under Augustus and Tiberius, the time of the church between the ascension and the parousia, and finally the time of universal judgment when "there shall be time no longer . . . when the mystery of God shall be finished" (Rev 10:6-7). We have no right to introduce our linear conception of time into the heavenly vision of the mystery. The nature of the heavenly view of reality is concealed from us, but it is revealed to us through the liturgical experience of the church. Every prophetic vision of the mystery of the redemption tends to superpose and merge the periods which we separate in their historical development.[4]

The heavenly priesthood of Christ constitutes the very heart of the mystery; it is the heavenly, extra-temporal representation of the redemption in history. The two planes (historical and celestial) are inseparable, but a distinction must be drawn between them. It was on earth that the son of God fulfilled his sacrifice; but it is in heaven that his sacrifice is accepted, for the final end of the paschal drama is our Father

4. See the prophecies of the Old Testament, the words of Jesus concerning the destruction of Jerusalem and the end of the world, and also the apocalyptic visions of St. John which are incapable of transposing literally in the historical framework of our present life.

who is in heaven. It is in this heavenly perspective that the whole of Christ's ministry on earth must be contemplated.

> Jesus was slain on Golgotha, but it was beneath the tabernacle of heaven that he offered his blood as our priest. The offering presupposes the sacrifice. The doctrine in Hebrews does not abandon Golgotha; but the priestly ministry of Christ (which is emphasized through this sacrifice) is related not to Golgotha but to the tabernacle of heaven. The two factors are closely linked. But the death of Jesus on the cross was accomplished at a definite time and place; Golgotha is part of history. The heavenly sanctuary is beyond time and space. One can only speak conditionally of the heavenly tabernacle as the "place" where Christ's sacrifice took place. But the temporal and the extra-temporal are given in an indivisible unity in the epistle to the Hebrews.[5]

Christ's sacrifice is therefore accomplished once for all, it is perfect and complete and has been accepted by the Father; Pentecost is the undoubted sign of this. But Christ's death takes all its meaning from the perspective of the holy sacrifice for ever offered by Christ. His priestly intercession for sinners remains for always.[6]

But the theme of Christ's *heavenly priesthood* (contained in Hebrews) by no means covers the whole of Christ's eternal mediation for men. The epistle to the Hebrews uses the

5. Mgr. Cassien, *Christ and the first christian generation* (Paris, 1950), p. 270 (in Russian).

6. Calvin has clearly shown the celestial element in the redemption: "Everything which seems at first sight to be earthly in Christ must be considered spiritually, with the eyes of faith. His flesh, which he took from the seed of Abraham, will then be seen to have come to life because it was the temple of God. Even his death brought life to all men, which is certainly a supernatural thing. Thus the Apostle does not merely regard the quality of his human nature, but rather the secret virtue of the Holy Spirit, which is the reason why there is nothing earthly about the death of Christ. The shedding of his blood was eternal; but the purgation (of sins) was internal and spiritual. In short, he died on earth, but the virtue and effectiveness of his death came from heaven" (on Hebrews 8:2-4). (Quoted by Spicq, *op. cit.*, p. 315, note I).

word "forerunner" to describe the heavenly high priest: "Within the veil . . . the forerunner is for us entered, even Jesus, made a high priest for ever after the order of Melchizedek" (Heb 6:20). This passage expresses a truth which is of the utmost importance for an understanding of Christian worship, namely that it was not only in his capacity as high priest, but also as "forerunner for us" that Jesus entered heaven.[7] By penetrating within the holy of holies, he draws us after him into the intimacy of the life of the Trinity, which had hitherto been inaccessible to fallen mankind, into the very heart of the divine glory, of which the biblical image was the holy of holies in the temple at Jerusalem. A solemn procession is formed, and a whole cloud of witnesses rises up to follow Christ glorified (cf. also Heb 12:12-14; 13:14; 1 Thess 4:17).

> The Son and the sons walk together, as associates in the same enterprise ("partakers of Christ," Heb 3:14), like a Shepherd and his sheep (Heb 13:20). They form a single group as they march forward. The high priest's entry into God's presence must therefore be regarded as the entry of a forerunner (Heb 6:20). He traces the path, he goes ahead to inaugurate and consecrate it (Heb 10:19-20). The believers have only to follow him in order to enter heaven themselves also. . . .[8]

The place set aside for the formation of this procession is the church, the house of God, whose head is the high priest himself (Heb 10:21 ff.). It is centered in the eucharistic liturgy of the community, which is one with the heavenly offering of Jesus. The Eucharist is a liturgical projection of the heavenly worship presented by Jesus, the high priest; it is also the commemoration of Christ's sacrifice in history on the cross.

7. Cf. Mgr. Cassien, "Jesus le Précurseur" in *Theologia,* 27 (1956), Athens. Cf. also Congar, *op. cit.,* pp. 205-207.

8. C. Spicq, *L'Epître aux Hébreux,* Vol. 1 (1952), p. 301.

THE ASCENSION IN EUCHARISTIC WORSHIP

The eucharistic liturgy is the common act of the church through which it expresses its priestly vocation. In fact the church participates in the priestly mission of her divine bridegroom (cf. Ex 18:6; 1 Pet 2:5, 9; Rev 5:10). In the eucharistic service the whole church is associated with the sacrifice of Christ. Through the intermediary of the consecrated minister, the church is the high priest of the new faith, and intercedes for mankind *in Christo* before the throne of God. The worship of the Church therefore constitutes a liturgical and sacramental representation of the sacrifice on the cross and of the heavenly priesthood of Jesus, in which the two aspects of his ministry (earthly and heavenly) are commemorated and portrayed. Bishop Cassien writes: "The same correlation which exists between Christ's death on Golgotha and his sacrifice under the tabernacle beyond time and space—that same correlation must be affirmed between the heavenly sacrifice and the many celebrations of the Eucharist on earthly altars."[9]

The earthly aspect (the sacrifice of the cross and the resurrection) is commemorated in the memorial of the passion, in the minister's recital of Christ's last commandment ("do this in remembrance of me"), and in the repetition of the words pronounced by Christ when he instituted the Last Supper.

The heavenly aspect of Christ's sacrifice (his self-offering and his intercession before the throne of God) is no longer commemorated because, as we have seen, it transcends time and space. Not being situated in the past, it can only be the object of an invocation, an "epiclesis" addressed to the Father in heaven, in which the Church joins in the priestly intercession of Christ, praying God to bestow the Holy Spirit upon the gifts offered upon the altar, and upon the faithful

9. Mgr. Cassien, *op. cit.,* p. 272.

who surround the minister. The epiclesis, the invocation of the Holy Spirit, and the expectation of his coming, correspond in the history of the church to the ten days between ascension and pentecost when the apostles met in the temple (Lk 24:53) and in the upper room (Acts 1:13) and there awaited in joy the coming of the Comforter promised to them by Jesus.

These two aspects—commemoration and epiclesis—are indeed indivisible, but a distinction must be drawn between them, because it is the gift of the Holy Spirit which is the pledge that the Father has accepted the eucharistic offerings; and it is through the descent of the Holy Spirit that the unity of the Shepherd's flock is strengthened. Fortified with the pentecostal gifts, the flock moves forward towards the heavenly sanctuary, in the steps of the forerunner.

The heavenly dimension of the Orthodox liturgy springs from the very nature of the church. The church in its intimate nature is not merely an expectation of the kingdom of God; it is a foreshadowing of that kingdom already in existence now, on earth. By its very nature the church is placed between the two "aeons"—the old aeon of sin, under the domination of the powers of evil, in which we are still waiting and striving for the final victory of God—and the new aeon, when God's kingdom shall be consummated. Nevertheless it is undeniable that his kingdom is already present in the life of the church on earth.

"The church in the world," writes Olivier Clément, "is not merely a proclamation of God's kingdom, but a realization of it; nevertheless it is not of this world . . . The time of the church therefore culminates in the realization by every human being that the End is already present, and that history is already consummated in Christ."[10]

10. Olivier Clément, "Notes sur le Temps" (3rd part), *Messager de l'Exarchat du Patriarche russe en Europe Occidentale,* No. 28 (1957), p. 217.

The whole prayer of the church is therefore an invocation of the kingdom of God, a triumphant certainty that it is near, that it is within us, a call and an expectation of pentecost when, in response to Jesus' supplication (Jn 14:16) the Father pours out the living waters of the Holy Spirit upon the church. It is in the church's prayer that this present, radiant reality of the kingdom becomes eminently tangible.

"The whole of the church's charismatic life," says Father S. Bulgakov, "with its prayers, offices, sacraments, in which the grace of the Holy Spirit is always poured forth, belongs to the sphere of God's kingdom. As members of the church we penetrate into that kingdom and participate in it. . . ."[11]

This celestial dimension is expressed with remarkable constancy throughout the Orthodox liturgy. The Fathers of the church insisted upon this.[12] The liturgy re-creates for us the earthly life of the Word incarnate and his ascension in glory. It is not restricted, like the Latin Mass, to the accom-

---

11. S. Bulgakov, "On the Kingdom of God" in *La Voie,* No. 11 (Paris, 1928), p. 10 (in Russian). A just balance (!) must be kept between an excessive insistence on the heavenly and eschatological character of the kingdom already brought about, and an insistence on the other hand on the "not yet" of the kingdom of God here on earth. The royal priesthood of the church shows not only the reign of Christ over the church and his intercession for it, but also the real participation *from now onwards* of the church in the royal and priestly intercession of the Christ-Forerunner. We are reminded in this connection of both the narrative and the invocatory sense of the Hebrew words "Maranatha" ("Come, Lord" and "The Lord comes") and "Amen" ("It is so" and "So be it").

Here I would point to the article by Prof. J. J. von Allmen, "Worship and the Holy Spirit" in which the author describes the "eschatological play" which is Christian worship, "in the tension between the future which has already begun, with its glory, its freedom, its illumination, and the past which still endures—dark, enslaved and restricted."

12. "According to the traditional conception of the liturgy," writes Mme. M. Lot-Borodine, "this solemn office is only the earthly translation of the office celebrated in heaven by the angelic powers, led by the high priest after the order of Melchizedek, hence the name *theia* (divine) *liturgia*." *Un maître de la spiritualité byzantine au XIVe siècle: Nicolas Cabasilas* (Paris, 1959), p. 23.

plishment of the non-bloody sacrifice, pervaded by appropriate readings and prayers.[13]

In a classical work entitled *l'Explication de la divine Liturgie,* Nicolas Cabasilas, a great lay mystic of the fourteenth century in Byzantium, describes the symbolic meaning of the different eucharistic rites and prayers as follows:

> The psalmodies at the beginning [of the liturgy of the catechumens] indicate the first period of the redemptive plan; the biblical readings which follow indicate the second period. What precedes the sacrifice recalls what happened before the Lord's death: his coming, his perfect manifestation. The sacrifice commemorates the death of Christ, his resurrection and his ascension up to the moment when he transforms the precious gifts into the actual body of the Savior. The consecration which follows the act of sacrifice commemorates the promise of the Father, i.e., the descent of the Spirit upon the apostles, the conversion of the nations through the apostles, and the divine society.[14]

The liturgy of the "catechumens," or liturgy of the word, opens with the Trinitarian benediction: "Blessed be the kingdom of the Father and of the Son and of the Holy Spirit. . . ." The whole purpose of Christian worship is to bless the Trinity, and to proclaim aloud the coming of the kingdom to the ends of the earth.

The liturgy of the catechumens "is a slow constant movement of souls upward towards heaven"[15] culminating in the

13. L. Bouyer, "Les catholiques occidentaux et la liturgie byzantine," in *Dieu Vivant,* no. 21, p. 22.

14. Chapter 16, summary of the meaning of the Liturgy. Migne, *P. G.,* 150, col. 404 B. However, Father Alexander Schmemann has clearly demonstrated in his *Introduction to liturgical theology* (Paris, 1961, in Russian), how the "representative" symbolism of Byzantine commentators on the liturgy showing the meanings of the various parts of the liturgy in relation to redemption must be distinguished from the "synthetic" symbolism of the early church which made real in the eucharistic sacrifice the complete and indivisible mystery of Christ's death and resurrection.

15. M. Lot-Borodine, *op. cit.,* p. 33.

solemn procession with the Gospel and the singing of the *Trisagion* ("Holy God, Holy and Mighty, Holy and Immortal, have mercy upon us"). As Cabasilas writes, "this is the acclamation of the united choir composed of angels and human beings, welded into a single church through the manifestation of Christ who is both of heaven and of earth. That is why we sing this hymn after the ostension and entry (procession) of the Gospel, thus proclaiming that by coming among us Christ has placed us with the angels, and established us amid the angelic choirs."[16] The *Trisagion* is a Christian form of the chant "Holy, Holy" sung by the cherubim in Isaiah's vision (Is 6:3) and by the four beasts in the book of Revelation (Rev 4:8).[17] The liturgy refers many times to the singing of the *Sanctus,* which stresses the direct participation of the angels in the mystery of the Eucharist, and the unity of the church militant and triumphant centered in Christ glorified (represented on the altar). The angels surrounding the divine throne and continually praising God are invisibly present at the church's liturgy, with all the members of the church in heaven, gathered around the lamb.[18] That is why, during the prothesis (the preparation of the eucharistic elements), the officiating priest speaks not only of the living and the dead, but also of the members of the church triumphant, of the Virgin Mary, the saints and angels, thus commemorating the participation of the whole church in the heavenly sacrifice symbolized upon the altar.

As the solemn moment of the mysteries approaches, the

16. Nicolas Cabasilas, *op. cit., P. G.*, 150, col. 412 B - 413 A.

17. According to Byzantine tradition, the *Trisagion* hymn ("Holy God, holy and mighty, holy and immortal") was revealed to the Christians in Constantinople in the fifth century by angels. The Christians are said to have added the words "Have mercy upon us." (St. John of Damascus, *De fide orth.* I. III, chap. X, *P. G.*, 94, col. 1021 A).

18. "Lamb"—symbolic name given to the consecrated bread, recalling the sacrifice on the cross (Jn 1:29-36) and the celestial adoration of Jesus glorified in the vision of the book of Revelation (Rev 5:8-14).

priest invokes God's mercy and implores him to make us worthy to stand before his holy altar without reproach or condemnation, for the altar before which the priest stands is the seat of God's glory, though he is invisible to our bodily eyes.

The "liturgy of the faithful," or Eucharist, opens with the *grand entry,* a slow procession down the nave towards the sanctuary, in which the priest carries aloft the unconsecrated elements above his head. The chants sung at this moment are splendid and are excellent illustrations of our subject. The best-known is the one called the Cherubic Hymn:

> Let us, mystically representing the Cherubim, sing the thrice holy hymn in honor of the life-giving Trinity; let us lay aside all earthly cares, that we may receive the King of all things, invisibly escorted by the angelic hosts. Alleluia, alleluia, alleluia.

On Holy Saturday this hymn is replaced by a hymn drawn from the Liturgy of Saint James:

> Let all mortal flesh keep silence and in awe and trembling stand, laying aside all earthly thoughts; for the King of Kings and Lord of Lords cometh to be slain, and to give himself to be the food of the faithful. Before him come the archangels with the principalities and powers, the many-eyed Cherubim, and the six-winged Seraphim, veiling their faces, and crying "Alleluia, alleluia, alleluia."

Finally, at the time of the liturgy of the pre-sanctified, at the moment of the great entry of the priest with the consecrated elements, the choir intones this hymn:

> Now the powers of heaven with us invisibly do minister. For lo! the king of glory entereth now. Behold the mystical sacrifice, all accomplished, is ushered in. Let us with fear and love draw near, that we may become partakers of life everlasting. Alleluia, alleluia, alleluia.

These three hymns, and other secret prayers, mention the

common theme of the invisible presence of the angelic powers (mystically represented by the believers) which accompany the king of glory as he mounts the altar of sacrifice. This theme of the presence of the angels and their participation in the worship of the Christian congregation shows the extent to which the church is conscious of the indivisibility of the visible liturgy and the heavenly worship and how the whole church militant forms part of that heavenly adoration and of the ceaseless hymns sung by the angels and the church triumphant in praise of the lamb. The kingdom of the holy Trinity, the invisible presence of the angelic powers, the heavenly sacrifice, the propitiation before the sanctuary of the Father's glory, the expectation and the descent of the Holy Spirit upon the Christian congregation in a sacramental pentecost—these are the spiritual themes of the Orthodox liturgy, which is deeply anchored in the spirit of the New Testament as well as that of the early church.

After the grand entry and some prayers of intercession, comes the *anaphora,* opening with the traditional words of the ancient eucharistic liturgies: "Lift up your hearts" *(Sursum corda),* which means "Set your affection on things above, not on things on the earth" (Col 3:2). The faithful give their allegiance and declare that where their treasure is, there are their hearts also (Mt 6:21), there where Christ is seated on the right hand of the Father.[19] The church always commemorates the upward movement of the liturgy, through which earth and heaven meet. In the liturgy we participate in the one, eternal liturgy of heaven; and heaven itself stoops towards us and enfolds us, raising up our transfigured humanity to heaven. The whole of temporal time is sanctified and receives the value of eternity.

Father Alexander Schmemann writes:

19. Nicolas Cabasilas, *op. cit., P. G.,* 150, col. 424 D.

While the benediction and thanksgiving are found in nearly all the offices of the church, the exclamation "Lift up your hearts" belongs only to the Eucharist. The reason is that it is something more than an appeal to believers to fix their thoughts on things above. It reminds the church that *the Eucharist is fulfilled in heaven,* for "when we were dead in sins, God hath quickened us together with Christ (by grace ye are saved); and hath raised us up together, and made us sit together in heavenly place in Christ Jesus" (Eph 2:5-6). This rise of the church to heaven began with the little entry. Moreover in this case heaven means the kingdom of glory which was manifest in Christ. The liturgy is the eschatological sacrament, in the sense that what is accomplished in time, on earth, is a manifestation of what is heavenly and eternal, and enables us to participate in those heavenly things. "Heaven on earth" is the apparently paradoxical formula in which the Eastern Church has from the earliest times expressed this reality manifest in the liturgy as the sacrament of the age to come, the heavenly kingdom revealed on earth. Christ has entered into heaven itself (Heb 9:24), and our priestly acts will therefore always be the work of Christ "in heaven, although they are accomplished on earth" (St. John Chrysostom).[20]

With regard to the anaphora, I will mention the *Sanctus,* which is an integral part of the eucharistic prayer. It is the full expression of the song of triumph and praise sung by angels and men, the inhabitants of heaven and of earth. This song had already been sung before the Gospel-reading (Trisagion) and it was mentioned in the Hymn of the Cherubim accompanying the great entry ("Let us sing the thrice holy hymn").

During the singing of the *Sanctus* the priest says:

And we also, O Lord who lovest mankind, in company with these blessed Powers do cry aloud and say: Holy art thou, and all-holy thou, and thine only-begotten Son, and thy Holy Spirit; holy and all-holy; and majestic is thy glory, thou who hast so

20. Alexander Schmemann, "The Liturgy," in *Le Messager de l'Action chrétienne des Etudiants russes* (March-April 1952), p. 16 (in Russian).

loved thy world that thou gavest thine only-begotten Son (Jn 3:16).

Then follows the memorial of the work of Christ, and the account of the passion. After the words of institution come the epiclesis, the invocation of the Holy Spirit upon the faithful and upon the gifts placed on the altar. A true pentecost is accomplished at this moment when the Holy Spirit descends not only upon the gifts, consecrating them as the life-giving body and blood of our Lord, but also upon the whole congregation. Insufficient attention is paid to the fundamental importance of this descent of the Holy Spirit upon the church during the liturgy, to this invocation repeated several times by the priest between the consecration and the communion, that the Spirit may descend upon the people:

> Judge us worthy to find grace in thy sight, that our sacrifice may be accepted by thee and that the Spirit of thy grace may rest upon us, upon the gifts which we offer to thee, and upon all thy people.

The prayer which follows is particularly remarkable:

> Let us pray the Lord that our God, the lover of mankind, having received the precious gifts upon his holy, heavenly and spiritual altar, as a sweet-smelling savor, may in return send down upon us his divine grace and the gift of his Holy Spirit.

In all these prayers of intercession the theme of the descent of the Holy Spirit upon the believers recurs. The last prayer especially carries us into the spiritual atmosphere of the epistle to the Hebrews, into the setting of the celestial liturgy accomplished within the sanctuary of God. The gift of the Holy Spirit upon the elements and upon the faithful is the tangible pledge that the offerings of the church have been accepted upon the celestial altar as "an offering and a sacrifice to God for a sweet-smelling savor" (Eph 5:2), and that offering has become part of the sacrificial drama of the lamb; for the Spirit which now descends upon the gifts offered by the church is the same Spirit which descended upon the apostles in the upper room as a pledge of the Father's good will and his reconciliation through the sacrifice of his only Son; and it is the same Spirit by whose power the sacrifice of Christ has become an eternal propitiation (Heb 9:14), by whose power the Father has raised Christ to his right hand, and by whose power we also are raised to follow Jesus, the forerunner.

A word of dismissal follows, and to conclude the Eucharist I will quote Nicolas Cabasilas again:

> The sacrifice being ended . . . and all the rites of the divine service being completed, the priest seems to take leave after his audience with God and gradually to come from those heights through prayers, first within the sanctuary where he cannot be heard by the people, then leaving the sanctuary, standing in the midst of the people so that they can all hear him. . . .[21]

These few examples and quotations drawn from the liturgy of the Eucharist are sufficient to give a general idea of the heavenly perspective of the whole of Orthodox worship. As a Lenten prayer expresses it, "Standing in the temple of Thy glory, we believe that we stand in heaven . . ." As Saint Gregory of Palamas says, "Man illumined attains the summits of eternity . . . and already here on earth everything becomes miraculous. Even without being in heaven, he vies with the celestial powers in perpetual hymns of praise. In his life on earth he is like an angel, and he leads all creatures to God."[22]

Unfortunately we have to confine ourselves to the liturgy of the Eucharist, which is the center of the prayer of the

---

21. Nicolas Cabasilas, *op. cit., P. G.,* 150, col. 489 B.
22. St. Gregory Palamas, "Traité à la moniale Xénia sur les passions et la quiétude mentale" in Migne, *P. G.,* 150, col. 1081 AB.

church. But a deeper study of the daily office would abundantly confirm that it is always in the presence of, and in communion with, the angels and the whole church triumphant that the Christian congregation renders to God the ceaseless adoration which it owes him.[23]

THE ASCENSION, THE BASIS OF THE MISSIONARY WITNESS OF THE CHURCH

Taken as a whole, the prayer of the church is therefore a continual ascent of man towards intimacy with God, a procession upwards in the steps of Jesus the forerunner, towards the Father. This ascension culminates in the divinization of human nature, not only in the life beyond but *here and now*. The climax of this divinization is the eucharistic communion in which God himself becomes our food and transforms us through union with himself.

But Christ's ascension, in which we participate here on earth (Eph 2:4-6; Heb 12:22-24) has nothing in common with the individualistic ascensions of the privileged *illuminati* in Platonism, the Greek mysteries or the religions of India. They are all achieved through solitary contemplation, they are "a flight from the alone to the Alone,"[24] they are a series

---

23. Here are some examples of the hymns sung at Matins during Lent:

"With all the heavenly powers we cry, like the cherubim, singing the Trisagion hymn: Holy, holy, holy art Thou, O God, through the intercession of Thy incorporeal spirits, have mercy upon us."

"Echoing the celestial powers, we on earth present a hymn of victory to thee, O Thou who art good: Holy, holy art Thou, O God . . . "

"We mortals venture to offer to Thee the hymn sung by Thy spiritual servants, singing: Holy, holy, holy . . . "

"O Thou who wast contained within the Virgin's womb, without separating Thyself from the Father, grant O Christ, our God, that we may join Thy angels in crying to Thee: Holy, holy, holy, art Thou, O God . . . "

"Having our hearts in heaven, let us echo the angelic host and prostrate ourselves in fear before the Incorruptible One, crying to Him without ceasing the song of victory: Holy, holy, holy art Thou, O God . . ."

24. Plotinus, *Ennead* VI, tr. 9, c. 9 and 11; tr. 7, 3. 34.

of escapes leading farther and farther away; a forgetting and a denial of material things (which are regarded as evil, or as having no existence), a form of disincarnation. Such ascensions are achieved either through asceticism and ecstasy, or through philosophy, or through initiation into secret rites, in a context of endless transmigrations.[25]

Amid all these conceptions of salvation as escape, the Christian doctrine of the ascension alone is connected with a divine purpose for the world itself, which "God loved so much . . ." (Jn 3:16). The Christian ascension alone is based on a complete plan for the salvation of the world and on the presence of Christ glorified in the church, that presence being realized through the Holy Spirit in his different gifts of grace, a mysterious but real presence perceptible to the purified senses. The Christian ascension alone precedes the descent of God's Spirit upon the church, thus importing a celestial dimension into its liturgical and sacramental life, and conditioning the church's missionary witness in the world. "He that descended is the same also that ascended up far above all heavens, that he might fill all things," says Saint Paul (Eph 4:10), that he may fill all things *through his life-giving presence, in the Holy Spirit.*

Father Daniélou writes, "It is only through his ascension above the heavens that Christ can fill all things. It is only through being raised above the whole creation that his grace can be poured out upon the whole creation."[26]

For the ascension of Christ, and our liturgical and sacramental ascension inaugurated through the mystery of divine worship, is not a means of escape from this world. On the contrary, it is only by lifting up our hearts, by participating

25. Cf. H. de Lubac, *Catholicisme* (Paris, 1947), Chap. V, "Le christianisme et l'histoire, doctrines d'évasion," pp. 107-110. (Eng. trans.: *Catholicism,* New York, 1958.)
26. J. Daniélou, *op. cit.,* p. 166.

in the procession in the steps of the great priest and fore-runner, and by penetrating into the vision of intimacy with God, that we can bear authentic witness of "that which was from the beginning, which we have heard, which we have seen with our eyes, which we have looked upon, and our hands handled, of the Word of life; for the Life was manifested . . ." (1 Jn 1:1-2).

> The appeal [to lift up our hearts] is therefore not so much an appeal to detach ourselves from the world, but rather to remember the nature of the church and the purpose of the eucharistic gathering: "What has heaven to do with me?" said Saint John Chrysostom, "when I am contemplating the Lord of heaven, and becoming heaven myself?" As Jesus promised, "If a man love me . . . my Father will love him, and we will come unto him, and make our abode with him" (Jn 14:23). This appeal is also a demand. For those who remain on earth ("Let us be afraid of remaining on earth," says Chrysostom again) there is no place in this celestial Eucharist, and then our very presence is imputed to us as condemnation. When the choir, as the mouth-piece of the whole congregation, replies, "We lift up our hearts unto the Lord," our judgment is accomplished. For we cannot turn our hearts to the Lord at that moment unless our hearts are fixed on him throughout our lives, and unless we always measure earthly things by the standards of heaven. . . .[27]

Missionary witness is based on personal experience of the life of the church. And that experience depends on the vision, the encounter with Christ, who while present in our midst does not cease at the same time to be seated at the right hand of the Father. The biblical themes of the ascension and of Christ's celestial priesthood constitute in the first place a theological category which is an essential part of the liturgical life of the church. They form the basis of an Orthodox theology of evangelism, of the pastoral ministry, and of the whole mediation of the church in the world as a royal priest-

27. A. Schmemann, *op. cit.*, p. 16.

hood. There is an inner link between the two dimensions—liturgical and missionary. They reflect the nature of the church itself which has two aspects: 1) its life of prayer through which it reaches out towards encounter with Christ glorified in an irresistible impulse of worship; 2) its task of permeating earth with heaven, and raising everyone to his eternal destiny. If the church's life of prayer is not enclosed, but aims to spread throughout the world, the church's mission can be none other than to raise up all men to worship the holy Trinity.

Liturgy or Cult: Source or Resource?

MASSEY H. SHEPHERD, JR.

The New Testament perspective upon liturgy and worship persisted throughout the patristic age. If we may cite Dean Schmemann, "The Fathers do not 'reflect' on liturgy. For them it is not an *object* of theological inquiry and definition, but rather the living source and the ultimate criterion of all Christian thought."[1] It is worth noting that there exist no treatises on "liturgics" as such from the patristic period. There are works on prayer and the spiritual life, and catechetical instructions on the sacraments delivered to the newly baptized. These have to do with the normal and necessary pastoral ministry of the church. But the liturgy viewed as a definable, distinct category of religious phenomena is absent from the purview of the ancient Fathers.

One might bring forward as exceptions the "customaries" of the early church, the documents known as Church Orders, beginning with the *Didache* and Hippolytus' *Apostolic Tradition*. These were manuals that covered the whole range of what we would today call "practical theology." But their purpose was certainly not to isolate the liturgy from the more ordinary, or as we should say "secular," round of daily Christian living, but to direct the totality of Christian life in ways of sound tradition.

It is well-known how difficult it is for scholars to decide

1. Massey H. Shepherd, Jr., *Worship in Scripture and Tradition* (Oxford University Press, 1963), p. 167.

whether the thanksgivings before and after meals in the *Didache* (chaps. ix-x) refer to the eucharistic sacrament or to the agape fellowship meal. In the unmistakable reference to the Eucharist (chap. xiv) as "a pure sacrifice," the author or compiler does not refer to the nature of the bread that is broken or to the ritual of thanksgiving that is offered, but to the reconciliation of the worshipers who participate. It is the love and forgiveness of Christian brothers that assure that "the sacrifice is not profaned" (literally, "made common"), and so is fulfilled the prophecy that "in every place and time a pure sacrifice shall be offered unto me, for I am a great King, says the Lord, and my Name is wonderful among the peoples" (Mal 1:11, 14).

In Hippolytus' treatise there is certainly a clearer distinction between the Eucharist and the agape, not only in the manner of celebration, but in their respective obligatory or voluntary character. Yet Hippolytus uses the Pauline phrase "the Lord's Supper" to denote the agape (chap. xxvi)! He insists that the unbaptized are not to participate in the table grace of the agape, but to have their separate thanksgiving. This injunction reveals in particular the difference in outlook of the ancient church from that of the church today. In the ancient church the real dividing line between the realm of redemption and the realm yet to be redeemed was Baptism, not a disciplinary admission to communicant—that is, cultic—status.

Churchmen today would be horrified at the thought that unbaptized persons should not be permitted to eat at the same table and share the same table grace at our ordinary church suppers. We even welcome them to participate in the church's public prayers; though, of course, we exclude them, along with our own baptized but unconfirmed children, from receiving Communion. Otherwise we let them share in all the benefits and blessings of the rest of our rites. Such a practice would have been inconceivable in the patristic church, which allowed the unbaptized to be present only at the readings of the Scriptures and the sermon—the kerygmatic and missionary introduction of the liturgy. Before any prayer was offered they were dismissed.

I do not believe that the original motivation of this practice was due to any cultic distinction of the sacred and the profane, though it may have entered into consideration in the later patristic age. It was due rather to the clear conviction of the early church that the baptized had entered into another realm of existence—the Age to Come. They took the prayers of the liturgy with utmost realism, and with a sense of their corporate force, that startles the pervasive individualistic thinking of our times. That is to say, they considered it impossible for one who had not professed Christ to participate in prayer in his name; and one could not merely be present and watch the proceedings. For only those with faith really knew what was taking place. They did not consider the liturgy a means of instruction.

The same thinking lies behind the universal custom of the ancient church, even after the cultic sense of liturgy began to take hold, of never explaining the meaning of the sacramental mysteries during the preparation of the catechumens. All the patristic lectures on the sacraments—the so-called "mystagogical lectures"—were delivered to the new converts *after* and not before they were initiated at the Easter rites.[2] This again would seem foolish to our modern ways of thinking and doing. Not many clergy today would risk withholding instruction on the meaning of Baptism, Confirmation, and Eucharist until after the class of candidates had participated in them. But then, the early church did not understand the liturgy as an object of knowledge but as a subject

---

2. We possess such courses of lectures from Cyril of Jerusalem, Theodore of Mopsuestia, John Chrysostom, and Ambrose.

of experience. One could not understand what one had not experienced, no matter how many lectures were given and instructional exercises imposed. The liturgy can only be known from the inside, since it is the very frame of the new total existence with Christ "in the heavenly places" (Eph 1:3, 20).

The ancient church did not practice the so-called *disciplina arcana* because of a fear of profaning what was sacred. In fact, apologetic writers were quite prepared to describe Christian worship to pagan readers, with a view toward showing its ethical and spiritual character. They were reticent simply for the reason—so often given by Origen, for example, in his sermons—that the unbaptized would not really know what they were talking about.[3] The liturgy is a mystery known only to the faithful in this sense. It is not a secret, like the cults of the mystery-religions. It is a new order of eschatological existence, which those still living in the old *aeon* cannot possibly comprehend, until they have died and been raised to newness of life in Christ.

Another passage in Hippolytus is apropos of our point—namely, the well-known reference, first of its kind, to "fasting communion" (chap. xxxii):

> Let every one of the faithful be careful to partake of the Eucharist before he eats anything else. For if he partakes with faith, even though some deadly thing were given him, after this it cannot hurt him.

The injunction occurs with directions about the daily reception of the sacrament by the laity from consecrated bread taken home from church—a custom that obtained in North

---

3. On the *disciplina arcana,* see the bibliography listed in E. Bourque, *Etude sur les sacramentaires romains,* I (Studi di antichità cristiana XX; Rome, 1948), p. 1, to which may be added P. Batiffol's article "Arcane," *Dictionnaire de théologie catholique,* I, 1738-58. I find myself in agreement with Abbé Bourque that recent discoveries have demonstrated how restricted was the "field of the law of the arcana."

Africa and possibly also in Rome (if Hippolytus is really Roman) during the third century. This practice would shock churchmen today, who would consider it very remiss for the laity to possess the reserved sacrament and communicate themselves from it. We will not even allow laymen to administer Communion in church under the eye and supervision of the clergy. Is this itself an indication of how we have, apart from all canonical questions of appropriate discipline, clericalized and sacralized the sacrament?

Be that as it may, Hippolytus' directive does suggest that he views the consecrated Eucharist as a kind of *sacrum,* at least when it is received in faith. But one should note carefully the reason he gives for receiving the Eucharist each day before taking other food. It is not a cultic reason—such as one usually hears today in defense of "fasting communion," namely, that it is an act of honor to our Lord to receive his body and blood before we have "profaned" our stomachs with other food—from God's good creation. Hippolytus is not interested in the honor of the sacrament but in the wholeness of the believer. The Eucharist sanctified the recipient so that no "deadly thing" *(mortale quodcumque)* could harm him. By deadly thing he is obviously thinking of anything that might happen to a Christian to bring about not only physical but also spiritual death. The point is not so much the sacrosanctness of the eucharistic species, though that is implied, but the sacredness of the total daily life of the Christian in what our Prayer Book calls "all the changes and chances of this mortal life."

It is not possible to point to any exact time or occasion when the church began to look upon the liturgy as a cult. That it should come to do so was no doubt inevitable, once it recognized and accepted the fact that sin exists in the fellowship of believers no less than in the world outside, that the church is a mixed society of wheat and tares that will not be finally separated until the last judgment. Thus, for example, we understand the gradual shift in meaning of such a word as *saint* from a definition of each and every baptized person to a specialized connotation of the more distinguished witnesses to the faith. Thus in the Creed, there is an ambiguity in the phrase "The Communion of Saints"—whether "saints" refers to persons or to things, to the whole community of the redeemed, or whether it is intended to refer to the holy and sacral mysteries and actions in which the redeemed are privileged to share.[4]

It is perhaps unfair to make Ignatius of Antioch the villain who first introduced the cultic point of view with his extravagant metaphor about the eucharistic bread as "the medicine of immortality, the antidote that we should not die but live forever in Jesus Christ."[5] Ignatius was full of extravagant metaphors. His description of the Eucharist is only his stylistic way of stating the eschatological dimension of the sacrament. In his letter to the Romans, he described his own martyrdom in eucharistic terminology, quite after the manner of speaking in the New Testament: "I am God's grain, and am ground by the teeth of wild beasts, that I may be found pure bread."[6]

4. The traditional view that "Communion of Saints" refers to persons is ably supported by J. N. D. Kelly, *Early Christian Creeds* (Longmans, Green and Co., 1950), pp. 388-97. For the opposite view—that it refers to the sacraments—see the dissertation of Istvan Benkö (who follows his teacher Oscar Cullmann), *Sanctorum communio* (Basel, 1951), and my review of this work in *Review of Religion* XIX (1955), 212-14. A good illustration of our point is the way the medieval church misunderstood the primary meaning of the Festival of All Saints, and followed it by the institution of "All Souls." But, as the late Professor B. S. Easton said so aptly, "in Anglican tradition 'All Saints' is 'All Souls' as well; this accords better with the New Testament doctrine of 'sainthood.' " B. S. Easton and H. C. Robbins, *The Eternal Word in the Modern World* (Scribners, 1937), p. 297.

5. *Ephesians* 20:2.
6. *Romans* 4:1.

A better case could be made for apologists such as Justin Martyr and Tertullian, who saw the analogies between the Christian sacraments and the pagan mystery rites. Justin distinctly says that the bread and drink are not "common" once they have received thanksgiving by "the word of prayer that comes from him," that is, from the Logos.[7] On the other hand, Justin's pupil Irenaeus used the same kind of language to refute the Gnostic heresy in its denial of the essential goodness of the created order of God; and he was horrified by the Gnostic treatment of sacraments as esoteric and magical instruments of grace.[8]

Another factor in the changing point of view was the typological application to the sacraments and the ministry of the church of the whole cultic vocabulary of the Old Testament. Thus priestly and sacrificial terms came to be used of the clergy and of the rites over which they presided; and a distinction was made—unknown to the New Testament—between *kleros* and *laos,* clergy and laity, which has been with us ever since.[9] A recent study of Cyprian has attempted to show that this worthy Father of the church was unfortunately advanced to the episcopate too soon after his conversion and without proper education in the church's tradition of teaching. For it was Cyprian who exalted the potency of the eucharistic species to work physical harm upon unworthy communicants, and who initiated the ten-

7. *Apology,* I, 66.

8. *Against Heresies* iv. 17. 5; iv. 18.6; v. 2. 2-3.

9. The tendency seems to have started with I Clement (cf. chap. 40), but it is not established usage to refer *laos* to the nonordained "laity" until Clement of Alexandria (*Stromata* iii. 12. 90) and Tertullian (*Prescriptions against Heretics* 41). But when Tertullian passed over to Montanism, he rejected the distinction; cf. his famous tirade in *An Exhortation to Chastity* 7: "For are not we lay people also priests? . . . It is ecclesiastical authority which distinguishes clergy and laity, this and the dignity which sets a man apart by reason of membership in the hierarchy. . . . Obviously, where there are three gathered together, even though they are lay persons, there is a church."

dency to define the church by reference to the hierarchy.[10]

The fourth and fifth centuries witnessed an intensification of the paradox, that as the church became more and more involved in responsibility for the sanctification of the total life of society, it sharpened the distinction between the sacred and the profane. Many delayed their baptism even to the point of death, lest they defile the holy remission of guilt by post-baptismal sin. (It should be said, however, that responsible church leaders were not very happy about this custom.) In the case of the Eucharist, more and more emphasis was placed upon the awesomeness of the miracle of consecration. The invocation of the Spirit was now summoned upon the elements instead of upon the church. One must approach them like Moses before the burning bush, and gaze in dread before the fire of divine Presence that makes the elements as it were "live coals" upon the altar.[11] It is no wonder that the people were more and more discouraged from communicating, despite the exhortations of the clergy, and that the consecration of the mysteries was finally withdrawn from sight behind curtains and closed screens.

One could draw innumerable illustrations of the changing perspective. A good one to consider is the development of cultic places. We have noted that the primitive church had no sacred place of meeting—no word for a sacred building or temple consecrated for cult purposes. Indeed the church has never lost entirely the sense of the appropriateness of using any place, outdoors or indoors, above or below ground, for the celebration of the liturgy, wherever it can assemble its members. The "house-church" is still a reality among us. We know from the apologists that one of the reasons for

10. M. F. Wiles, "The Theological Legacy of St. Cyprian," *The Journal of Ecclesiastical History* XIV (1963), 139-49.

11. The tendency is very marked in Chrysostom, and his friend and contemporary, Theodore of Mopsuestia. See the apt remarks of Dom Gregory Dix, *The Shape of the Liturgy* (Dacre Press, 1944), pp. 480-85.

popular charges of atheism against Christianity in the early centuries was its lack of proper temples and cult edifices.[12] It is characteristic that Christian usage has applied the word *church* to any gathering place where the church comes together.

Even after the church was able to erect special buildings for its liturgical use during the long peace that extended between the Valerian and the Diocletian persecutions, the old terminology was maintained. Lactantius, for example, consistently speaks of the church buildings destroyed in the last great persecution as *conventicula*, "meeting houses," for the true temple of God *(dei templum)*, said he, consisted of church people themselves.[13] After Constantine began the construction of magnificent edifices for the church, the word adopted for them was *basilica*, "royal house," taken from the secular rather than from the cultic vocabulary of the age.

Ultimately, however, the church developed a special form of the liturgy for consecrating church buildings, other than a dedication of them simply by the celebration of worship. The medieval orders of consecration of churches involve ceremonies of anointing and sprinkling with holy water as though the buildings were themselves being baptized and confirmed! Our own Prayer Book "Form of Consecration of a Church or Chapel," adopted in 1799, is to say the least an ambiguous compromise between a regular celebration of divine worship and a setting apart of the building "from all unhallowed, worldly, and common uses." But the prayer of consecration does recall the denunciation by the first martyr, St. Stephen, of the Jewish temple, by reference to the prophetic word that the Most High "whom the heaven of heavens cannot contain" can "much less" be contained in "walls of temples made with hands" (cf. Acts 7:48-49).

13. *On the Death of the Persecutors* 15.
12. Minucius Felix, *Octavius* 32; Clement of Alexandria, *Stromata* vii. 5. 29.

It is, of course, a natural and appropriate instinct to show reverence to the places which by long association have been the focus of encounter with the living God and his word and grace. But it can be carried to exaggerated extremes. Sitting as I do on the architectural commission of my diocese, I discover how difficult it is to persuade church building committees, who are planning the so-called "multiple purpose" structure—which will probably be torn down or entirely reconstructed before it is ever "consecrated"—that it is unnecessary to provide a screen or curtain to be drawn across the "sanctuary" when they wish to use the nave for "unholy" purposes such as parish meetings or dinners. For why should the sight of the holy table and its furnishings be considered unfitting when the church assembles to live its common life of work and mission? Certainly whatever is proper and fitting for Christian people to do together is proper and fitting for them to do in the presence of the "holy place."

There is a danger, one might say a blasphemous danger, in this cultic attitude toward the "holy place." There are, alas, some congregations that have so surrounded not only the building but the very liturgy that is celebrated within it with such taboos of what is thought to be seemly that they are unable to welcome in their midst baptized persons of other races or classes than themselves. And the converse of this is true also. There are parishes that would not dare to draw this distinction in the "holy place," but are prepared to draw it in the supposedly "unholy place" where other parish activities than those of worship take place. This, too, is blasphemy—to allow the outcast to eat of the bread and drink of the cup at the altar but not to invite him to partake of the agape in a sandwich and a cup of coffee.

One of the consequences of turning the liturgy into a cult is that it becomes one among many objects that can be used for illustration and teaching of religion. Worship is made

one among many, even though it may be the most important, resources for instruction in the faith. We inherit this
approach to the liturgy from the middle ages. For example,
the Western Church was unable to comprehend the theological significance of the iconoclastic controversy, and set-
tled for the principle that liturgical art is not sacramental but
decorative. Images and pictures are merely external vehicles
for communicating a set of truths; they are the "Bible of the
unlettered." The same notion was applied to the ceremonies
of the liturgy; they were externalized as instructive instruments. Medieval treatises on the liturgy are full of this sort
of thing—the allegorizing of the liturgy to teach doctrine
and morals.

A typical example of this approach may be taken from the
treatise on the liturgy entitled *Gemma animae* ("The Jewel
of the Soul") by Honorius of Autun (d. *ca.* 1150):

> The Mass imitates the conflict of a certain battle and triumph of
> victory. . . . Jesus our Emperor has fought with the devil and
> obtained for men the celestial republic that had been destroyed
> by enemies. . . . For the procession of the pontiff, clergy, and
> people is, as it were, the setting out of the Emperor and his
> army to war. They are attired with albs underneath and copes
> over them, or other solemn vestments, as soldiers about to fight
> who are protected with leather breastplates underneath and
> shields above them. When they go out from the choir they pro-
> ceed as from a royal court. As the imperial banner and standard
> are borne in front by standard-bearers, so before us the cross
> and banner are carried. There follow, like two armies, the
> singers advancing in order. Among them go instructors and pre-
> centors just as leaders of cohorts and inciters to war.[14]

So Honorius goes on with interminable illustration. Another
of his interesting instructions is a comparison of the Mass to
a judicial proceeding in a public court before judges. All of
this was certainly a lively translation of the liturgy into the
vernacular of the common life of the age. We should not

14. i. 72 (*P.L.* CLXXII, 566).

throw stones. All of us have done the same kind of translation: for example, the way we use the offertory of the Eucharist to illustrate the economic and political order of our times in and by which men make, distribute, buy, and sell bread and wine. Such instructions no doubt have their uses and values.

In a pamphlet published several years ago by our church's national Department of Christian Education, entitled *Family Corporate Worship,* we were given this catechetical sample of question and answer:

> Q. Why is Family Corporate Worship important to the Christian Education program?
> A. This practice is necessary to the religious life of the home. It is a significant factor in the Christian education of children as well as their parents. In the repetition, week after week, of the services of the Book of Common Prayer throughout the Christian Year, worshipers are continually confronted with the major basic biblical doctrines and teachings of the Christian faith. Without the family pew, the church school courses . . . will be deprived of their liveliest access to the resources of the church.

This piece is as true and as misleading as was the pedagogical reason Archbishop Cranmer gave in the Prayer Book for the appropriateness of public baptism—namely, that every man present would be thereby reminded of his own profession made to God in his own baptism. Obviously this is true. No one would deny it. But the purpose of the liturgy is not primarily one of instruction and edification—as this pamphlet comes dangerously close to implying.

Let it be said at once and unequivocably that the liturgy is an inexhaustible source of edification. I say *source,* not *resource.* For it is not one object of our reverent attention and use, however important and significant. The liturgy is the subject of God's own invisible action and working. In the liturgy God acts not only upon the church but upon the whole world by his testimony to the accomplished work of Christ. This action is far deeper than our minds can consciously fathom or comprehend. In the liturgy the kingdom is being brought into realization, and we are captured by it. The wall of separation is removed, sin is forgiven, the dead are raised up and made alive in the Spirit. Our response in contemplation of this "mystery" is indeed edification—that "mystery hidden for ages in God who created all things; that through the church the manifold wisdom of God might now be made known to the principalities and powers in the heavenly places. This was according to the eternal purpose which he has realized in Christ Jesus our Lord, in whom we have boldness and confidence of access through our faith in him" (Eph 3:9-12).

If we set out, however, with the notion that the liturgy is a "significant factor" in an education program and the "liveliest access to the resources of the church," we risk making it subject to a standard or norm outside of itself, whether this be the Bible, or the faith considered as a set of doctrines, or perhaps some particularly idealized way of life. This was the disastrous trap into which the Reformation fell.

Having struggled valianty to remove the old categories of "sacred" and "profane," the Reformers then proceeded to ecclesiasticize the liturgy again by making it subject to a norm of right doctrine unto edifying. But since they could not agree just what this right doctrine of the Scriptures was, they fell into dispute about the liturgy—whether it should be fixed or free, whether this ceremony was superstitious or "dumb" and that one not. I would not say that the Reformers, any less than their medieval forebears, would have denied that the liturgy exists to glorify God and testify to the redemption of the world. But their bitter and sorrowful controversies over stinted prayers and dumb ceremonies reveal how primary was the concern to make the liturgy teach an orthodox doctrine and a right ecclesiastical practice. We sometimes forget how much hortatory material was scattered through the Reformation liturgies—much of it now providentially removed or ignored. If we approach the liturgy as a chief means of edification, we risk a new kind of clericalizing of it, since only the experts decide what is edifying. At the same time, we cannot prevent the people from making their own individual and individualistic choices of what is edifying.

If attendance upon the liturgy makes a man into a good and sound and orthodox churchman, well and good. But that is a by-product. The purpose of the liturgy is to draw us into that redeeming action of God whereby in Christ he reconciles the world to himself. The liturgy cannot, any more than God, be shut up in a box, protected from the profanities of the world. The liturgy is not just a church activity, or a complex of esoteric religious teachings, even though only the church celebrates it and only the man of faith understands it. It is open to the world, though the world acknowledge it not. It is celebrated for the world, though the world hold it in disrepute. The liturgy is God's mission to the world through his church, until all is made up that is lacking in the sufferings of Christ, until all that is scattered abroad is gathered together into one (cf. Col 1:24; Jn 11:52).

Yes, the church has an altar, as the author of Hebrews reminds us—not an altar like that of the old tabernacle, with its rigid taboos of what is clean and what is unclean, what is acceptable and what is burned without the camp. For our altar was itself raised up outside the gate, outside the camp.

> Therefore let us go forth to him outside the camp, bearing abuse for him. For here we have no lasting city, but we seek the city which is to come. Through him then let us continually offer up a sacrifice of praise to God, that is, the fruit of lips that acknowledge his name. Do not neglect to do good and to share what you have, for such sacrifices are pleasing to God (Heb 13:13-16).

The Mission of the People of God

DOUGLAS WEBSTER

I have recently been in the Middle East. You find there the people of God. You also find there missions. What for the most part you do not find is the mission of the people of God. The people of God exist in the ancient Eastern Churches surviving through the generations with their hierarchies, their customs, and their liturgies, scarcely changing. They have endured suffering and persecution on a scale that has seldom befallen the Western Church. For centuries now their energies have been chiefly spent in preventing their own faithful from becoming Muslims rather than in helping Muslims to become Christians. There are reasons for this, but they are not relevant here. The missions on the other hand are all foreign, Protestant and mostly American, or Catholic and mostly European. These too are the people of God, but they are not the people of the land; they represent a foreign church, not an indigenous one. They are in a sense an intrusion. Nevertheless, apart from this intrusion there would be virtually no Christian mission to Islam. This is the dilemma that arises when the concepts of mission and the people of God become divorced, whatever the cause. In our de-Christianized Europe a similar situation may well arise if the people of God ignore or forget or fail to discharge their mission.

In two recent books, the bishop of Woolwich writes of his

"growing conviction of the centrality of liturgy to evangelism."[1] Whilst wholly sharing this conviction, I want to supplement it with its corollary, the centrality of evangelism to liturgy. To insist on this and to offer some reasons for doing so is the theme of this paper.

We have all been learning the importance of giving equal weight to the ministry of the word and of the sacraments and admitting the dangers of exalting the one over against the other or at the expense of the other. It may be claimed that one of the fruits of the liturgical movement is that, in whichever direction we may have strayed, we have been brought back to a proper balance. Is it not time that the same recognition was given to the twin primary functions of the church, namely worship *and* mission, refraining from an emphasis on one to the exclusion of the other? On the continent, and particularly in the Roman Catholic Church, the liturgical movement seems to be much more aware of this necessary duality than is its Anglican counterpart. Liturgical renewal and missionary renewal are more inclined to go hand in hand. The two main chapters in Abbé Michonneau's book, *Revolution in a City Parish,* are entitled: "A Living, Apostolic Liturgy" and "A Missionary Apostolate." The concern is as much with what goes on outside the church as inside: how can it be otherwise with an apostolate whose function is to go and be outside? But the same burning passion for the mission outside is not always so discernible in our own movement. Is there not a risk of ecclesiastical self-consciousness in the very fun and novelty of liturgical movement innovations? How pleased the enlightened parish can feel with itself! How satisfying to be liturgically progressive and up-stage! Yet the test of it all is whether sinners are being brought to Christ. For the divine concern is with parish,

1. J. A. T. Robinson, *On being the Church in the World,* p. 63; *Liturgy Coming to Life,* p. 12.

people *and pagans*. On the Day of Judgment the manner in which we celebrated the liturgy is likely to be a matter of less moment than the efforts of priest and people to make Christ fully known in an unbelieving neighborhood and in the world beyond the parish boundaries.

In the volume, *The Parish Communion,* published twenty-five years ago, there are but two references to evangelism in more than 300 pages. This should make us pause to think. In comparison with the Roman liturgical movement, are we seeing sufficiently and clearly the mutuality of worship and mission, the implication of each for the other? Is Dom Gregory Dix right to say in his celebrated essay in the volume just mentioned: "In the primitive view the *raison d'être* both of the church and Eucharist is ultimately one thing only— *latreia,* worship, offered to God?" A similar remark is made by William Nicholls in his study of worship entitled *Jacob's Ladder,* whose opening sentence is: "Worship is the supreme and only indispensable activity of the Christian Church." Again and again statements like this are made, unqualified and unsupported by scriptural warrant. Are they true? In the days and years immediately after Pentecost can one imagine an apostle or an early Christian saying this kind of thing? Is there not far more in the New Testament about mission and witness and the proclamation of the Gospel than there is about worship? I am not for one moment suggesting that worship be dethroned from its primacy in the church's activities, but rather that we should recognize that it does not have a sole and unshared primacy. Surely the most outstanding difference between early Christianity and Judaism was that Judaism had become wrapped up in worship and had lost all sense of mission to the world, whereas the early Christians, taking for granted the supreme responsibility of offering worship to God which they inherited from Judaism, added to it a co-equal supreme responsibility of discharging the mission of God, which Judaism had failed to do. Their calling was to be witnesses as well as worshipers, apostles as well as disciples. The same Lord who before his passion gave the command "Do this," which instituted the church's Eucharist, before his ascension gave the command "Go," which instituted the church's mission. The doing and the going together constitute the being of the church. In many parishes and in some whole churches, whilst the one command is ceaselessly remembered and obeyed, the other is often forgotten and left. Yet the New Testament writers pay considerably more attention to the way in which the second of these commands was carried out, and that is why we have so much more information about the mission of the apostolic church than about its worship. Mission was not the second thought in that early church. It cohabited with worship as a dual concern, the glorious realities of worship driving those first Christians out into mission, the harsh realities of mission sending them back into worship, to enable them to go out once more.

This duality or shared primacy of worship and mission in the life of the church can best be understood as the Christian interpretation and expression of love. To love God with all one's being is to adore him in worship. But we are taught that this love for God is only real if it is inclusive of a love for our neighbors, and to love them is to be involved in mission and in service. Again, truly to love our neighbor is to want for him the best that life can offer, to want for him God and Christ, God's "gift beyond words." This love means mission. But the only hope of such mission being effective is to love and suffer and pray vicariously for our neighbor, to do what he will not do himself, to offer him vicariously to God. This love means worship. Thus mission and worship run in and out of each other. Both are expressions of the same energy moving in different directions—in worship to

God, in mission to man. They belong together because each is love.

It is notable that in the New Testament the same language sometimes is used to describe worship and to describe mission. Both are priestly activities, for both involve an offering, a liturgy, a service. St. Paul, as is well known, speaks of his Gentile mission in liturgical terms: "My priestly service is the preaching of the gospel of God, and it falls to me to offer the Gentiles to him as an acceptable sacrifice, consecrated by the Holy Spirit" (Rom 15:16, NEB). He actually refers to evangelism, preaching the Gospel of God, as priestly service. His Eucharist, his offering, is his converts. Writing to another group of Christians he speaks of his "sacrifice which is the offering up of your faith" (Phil 2:17, NEB). Again there is the vocabulary of proclaiming or showing forth the Lord's death. The same word which is used to describe the great proclamation of Christ in the Eucharist in 1 Corinthians 11:26 is used elsewhere of the proclamation of Christ in the Christian mission. Worship and mission are different ways of making the same proclamation, the one in and to the church, the other in and to the world, both indispensable. The church came into being as a result of the proclamation of the Gospel; the church lives by that proclamation and for it. Proclamation is central to its worship and to its mission. There is no either-or; it is all one.

William Nicholls reminds us that the biblical view of worship "is distinguished from all other religious understandings of the cultus by the fact that the worship of God's people in the Bible is always represented as the worship offered by those who have been redeemed." We may remind ourselves, however, that unless the church proclaims in its mission what it constantly proclaims in its worship, there will be no redeemed in the next generation to offer God worship. The celebration of the liturgy must mean a dedication to the mission. The true worshiper goes out of liturgy into mission, inevitably, for this is how he is to understand going out of the church into the bent and bungled world. The Christian's rôle in the world is to be a disturbing, interfering, missionary eruption, offering to wash feet that do not like being washed. This is the mission of the people of God. It flows directly out of the sanctuary, for only those who have knelt to receive the redeeming Christ will have the humility to kneel in service or the courage to stand in witness before the same principalities and powers which crucified him. Liturgy does not end at an ecclesiastical altar. It ends on altars outside the church, the places where we, like our Lord, get manhandled and hurt, rejected and misunderstood, because he has called us to be his witnesses as well as his worshipers. The altars before which we worship are the symbols of those other altars on which we are to suffer and pour out energy, if we join in the mission of the people of God, altars to be found in factories and on housing estates, in an African township, an Indian village, a Malayan jungle, a Japanese mob, or, to quote that strange verse, Revelation 11:8, "in Sodom and Egypt, where also their Lord was crucified." The language of worship and the language of mission are indeed the same. And often there is an ambiguity which may well be intentional, as in the very first words of the Anglican daily offices, "O Lord, open thou our lips; and our mouth shall shew forth thy praise." What better prayer for a Christian, whether as a prelude to his worship or to his witness?

This interchangeability of language and this duality of worship and mission are met with in the great passage about the people of God in 1 Peter 2. There is not time nor have I competence for detailed exegesis, and, as Selwyn's commentary shows, the divergences of interpretation have been notorious. But, at the risk of over-simplification, we may perhaps suggest that St. Peter is making statements about the nature and the function of the church—in other words, what the church is called to be and what the church is called to do. He does this with variations twice over, specifically in verses 5 and 9. Taking both verses together, the church is called to *be* "a spiritual house, a holy priesthood . . . an elect race, a royal priesthood, a holy nation, a people for God's own possession." This is how St. Peter describes and defines the people of God. But after both these groups of phrases on the nature of the church he appends a statement on what the church is called to *do*. In verse 5 its function as a priesthood is "to offer up spiritual sacrifices, acceptable to God through Jesus Christ." In verse 9 it is to "shew forth the excellencies of him who called you out of darkness into his marvellous light." The New English Bible renders this "to proclaim the triumphs of him . . ." Here again we find these two related ideas of offering and proclaiming. Some scholars are emphatic that there can be no eucharistic reference here, whilst others are equally convinced that there is. But are we compelled to choose? Selwyn (p. 295 f.) points out that these two final clauses in verses 5 and 9 are in the same category, and therefore "the offering of the spiritual sacrifices alluded to is identical with, or at least one form of, the proclamation of God's excellencies." He continues: "The sacrifices offered by the priestly body, the church, are intimately connected with the atoning work of Christ, and also serve to shew it forth in all its rich and reconciling mercy. He is presented as the center of a new sacrificial worship and a new sacrificial way of life. . . . Christians are to imitate Christ in his meekness, patience, and suffering, and they are to do it in order to win others to the faith—that is to say, to shew forth God's excellencies." Once more, then, we find the concepts of worship and mission in the life of the one people of God woven deliberately together. Its supreme

functions are "to offer up spiritual sacrifices" and "to proclaim God's triumphs" or excellencies. Both of these in their
completeness involve worship and mission, if we interpret
them in the light of the New Testament as a whole. And was
not Calvary itself at one and the same time the supreme act
of worship, giving basis and meaning to all our worship, and
the supreme moment of mission, giving basis and meaning
to the whole Christian mission?

I have deliberately given space to examining briefly this close
and fundamental relation between worship and mission in
the New Testament, first because I believe the liturgical
movement in Anglicanism may be in danger of losing sight
of this, and also because I think it is high time that someone
within the liturgical movement questioned the assertion and
assumption so frequently made that worship *alone* is the one
supreme activity of the church. I hope I have said enough
about the significance of worship to forestall the possible
criticism that I am underrating it in any way. My plea is
that worship and mission together should be regarded as the
supreme activities of the church on earth, as distinct from
the church in heaven, and my reading of the New Testament
compels me to say with Luther: Here I stand, I can no other.

If this does not lead me at once to the modern equivalent
of the Imperial Diet and a ban on all further utterance, we
may move on to a consideration of the meaning of the mission of the people of God.

In the incarnation God made himself visible, audible,
tangible, and vulnerable. He did this to redeem his people
and to make them the witnesses to, and the agents of, his
redemption for the whole world. The fact that the church is
in some sense the body of Christ means that through the
church he still wants to become visible, audible, tangible,
and vulnerable among men. And that means among unbe-

lievers. The cost of that mission to the Son of God was Calvary, where the mission of his life and the worship of his life were completed. (How much more effectively this truth might be transposed in our ritual if those who made it their custom to genuflect in the Nicene Creed at the incarnation were to remain genuflected for the crucifixion! Not to do so seems at least incongruous, for we were redeemed at Calvary, not Bethlehem.) The mission of the people of God will also demand sacrifice. In some places and at some time there will be "our lesser Calvaries." There is no mission without conflict, as almost every book in the New Testament makes clear.

If, therefore, the people of God become involved in the mission of the Son, sooner or later they will be involved in the passion of the Son. There are no signs that the twentieth-century world, with a population at least ten times as great as in our Lord's day, is any more kindly disposed to Jesus or the followers of Jesus than was the world of the first century. There are many more barbarians now than there were then; the difference is that today civilization includes them as it did not then. The mission of the people of God is so to live, whatever the cost or consequences, that the reality of Jesus Christ, as alive and active, saving and powerful, is sufficiently vivid and apparent for the unconvinced and unbelieving world to reckon with. The charge, "You shall be my witnesses," can hardly mean anything less. The inwardness of eucharistic worship, which is centered in the reality of Christ and of his sacrifice, should itself lead on to the outwardness of mission, the purpose of which is to make him visible today and the price of which is to bear our cross and to share his sacrifice.

We have concentrated much on the audibility of the Gospel; we have concentrated far less on the visibility of the Gospel. Yet salvation is something that has to be seen and shown as well as talked about. "All the ends of the earth shall *see* the salvation of our God," wrote Isaiah (52:10). "Mine eyes have *seen* thy salvation," said the old man Simeon. The mission of the church (in the words of St. Paul, Eph 3:9) is "to make all men see." Where else shall the world "see" Christ and the meaning of salvation except in the life of the people of God? But is the life of the people of God of such a quality that divine salvation is really visible there? And is it a salvation operative in all the varied contexts of our contemporary world? These are the crucial questions for the priest, the pastor, and the evangelist today. But the mission of the people of God remains the same in all situations. It is to confront the world in every possible way with Jesus Christ and his salvation.

What are these ways? We may consider four: by presence, by prayer, by proclamation, by transformation.

1. The presence of the people of God anywhere in the world is itself of missionary significance. There can be no mission without presence. But it must be an active and not a quiescent presence. In the Orthodox tradition of the Eastern Churches, mission has been thought of almost exclusively in terms of presence. A recent essay by a scholar of the Orthodox Church firmly relates the mission to the Eucharist and speaks of the Eucharist as transforming the church into mission, but he says nothing of how the church is to engage in mission.[2] Roman Catholic writers on missions are much more explicit about the purpose of the Christian presence. No one has stated this better than Charles de Foucauld, founder of the Little Brothers of Jesus, who regarded his vocation as that of "being present amongst people, with a

2. Alexander Schmemann, "The Missionary Imperative in the Orthodox Tradition," an essay in *The Theology of the Christian Mission*, edited by Gerald H. Anderson.

presence willed and intended as witness to the love of Christ."
His concept of mission was not that of a monastery with an
enclosed life offering certain services to the neighborhood,
nor that of a friary with permitted excursions into the world
for missionary purposes, but of an essentially lay community, living among and for and at the same level and
openly with their fellows, and occupied in the same jobs.
He saw that only in this kind of way could mission leap over
solid church frontiers and reach the otherwise unreachable.
A Roman Catholic writer in another volume tells how "in a
number of countries in Europe and America Catholic laymen find it better to carry on their work of witness outside
the Catholic organizations, in order to have more natural
opportunities of meeting non-Christians, and in order to
guard against the danger of creating a Christian world firmly
enclosed upon itself."[3]

This is presence with a purpose, and that purpose clearly
puts it in the category of mission. Mission by presence
should be the accepted vocation of all the people of God.
No qualifications are required for this, save that of being a
Christian. If evangelism in the technical sense is a specialist
activity with its own *charismata,* witness is an activity incum-
bent upon every instructed Christian. And whether he wishes
it or not, he is inescapably a witness if he is *known* to be a
Christian, and his witness is either good or bad. The presence of any Christian anywhere in the world is itself a fact
of missionary significance. The presence of Christ experienced in the Eucharist is the presence we are to express in
the world. He is to be met in the sacrament. He is also to be
met in the hungry and thirsty, the stranger and the naked,
the prisoner and the sick, in the neighbor on the road, and
in his little ones. Christians are to love him in the two dimensions of worship and mission and to meet him in both.

3. Roger Aubert in *Twentieth Century Christianity,* edited by Bishop
Stephen Neill, p. 64.

2. From presence follows prayer. An integral part of the mission of the people of God is to pray. Mission means intercession, and this, like the great intercession of the cross, is vicarious action. It is praying for those who cannot or will not pray for themselves. It is the other side of service, which is doing for them what they cannot or will not do for themselves. There can be no doubt whatever that contemplative communities whose whole life is given to prayer are indispensable to the Christian mission. Some of us would not dare to set foot overseas without the knowledge that we were being prayed for by those whose vocation this is. These are the specialists; the rest of us are also called to the work of prayer—as general practitioners, a bit amateur perhaps, not always very imaginative or inspired, but trying to be faithful.

Prayer belongs to the eucharistic action and to the missionary action of the church. But the church's prayer must range far beyond itself. However strong or ancient liturgical tradition may be in this connection, it is surely not enough to be invited to pray just for the whole state of Christ's church, whether or not we add "militant here on earth." Nor is it enough to pray only for "all *Christian* Kings, Princes, and Governors." When St. Paul gave instructions to Timothy that prayers were to be offered "for kings and all who are in high positions" (1 Tim 2:2, RSV), there were no Christian kings or governors. In much of the world this is still the case. Ought we not to ask those who are engaged in Prayer Book revision to give some thought to this? Cranmer and the compilers of our Prayer Book were living in a situation wholly different from our own in at least two respects. They were bounded by the concept of Christendom, which no longer exists, and like the rest of the Reformers they had no notion whatever of the church's missionary responsibility to the non-Christian world. Surely the time has come when the new situation, which is now nearly 200 years old, should be adequately reflected in our liturgical forms. The 1928 Prayer

Book makes an attempt to rectify this omission. The Church of South India Liturgy does this—and much else—a great deal better.

The same unawareness of mission is evident in some of our collects, which to most Anglicans are still sacrosanct and unimpeachable. Thus on the three great missionary festivals in our calendar, St. Andrew, the Epiphany, and the Conversion of St. Paul, the appointed collects have no explicit missionary reference. It is worth comparing them with the great improvements made by the Church of South India. On St. Andrew's day, the Prayer Book collect notes that he followed Christ without delay and asks that we "may forthwith give up ourselves obediently to follow thy holy commandments." The Church of South India collects notes that St. Andrew "obeyed the calling of thy Son Jesus Christ and brought others unto him," and asks that we "may be faithful disciples and witnesses of our Saviour Jesus Christ." On the Epiphany, the Prayer Book's petition in somewhat complicated language is "that we, which know thee now by faith, may after this life have the fruition of thy glorious Godhead." The Church of South India collect I quote in full: "Almighty God, who hast manifested thy Son Jesus Christ to be a light to the Gentiles, give us grace to declare his unsearchable riches in all the world, and to bring all men into the fellowship of thy religion, through the same Jesus Christ our Lord." On the Conversion of St. Paul, we pray with 1662 that "we, having his wonderful conversion in remembrance, may shew forth our thankfulness unto thee for the same, by following the holy doctrine which he taught." The Church of South India asks "that we who praise thee today for his conversion may by his example be moved to preach the gospel of thy grace, and finish our course with joy." I leave it to you to judge which of these alternatives is the more likely to help the people of God to become conscious of their mission. For while part of that mission is itself prayer, the very forms of the liturgical prayers themselves should create that awareness of missionary responsibility which the English Church in the sixteenth century, and for a long time afterwards, conspicuously lacked. The Anglican Communion will not be helped to fulfill its mission in the world if its liturgies continue indefinitely to retain a sixteenth-century outlook.

3. A third aspect of the mission of the people of God is proclamation. We have already given some attention to this. What is set forth and proclaimed in the Eucharist has to be set forth and proclaimed in the world. This is mission, and to fail at this point is to disclaim, which is what Simon Peter once did. It is by the continuous action of proclamation that the church grows. The apostolic church was an irrepressible church. "We cannot possibly give up speaking of things we have seen and heard" (Acts 4:20, NEB). That is why it multiplied. A Dutch scholar, in a recent book, has drawn attention to the fascinating parallelism between the Genesis command and the missionary command.[4] Twice in the early chapters of Genesis, to man at the end of the first creation story and to Noah after the flood, God gives the same command: "Be fruitful and multiply, and replenish the earth" (Gen 1:28; 9:1). But this is more than a command; it is an organic law permeating the whole of man's being. It is his nature to be reproductive. And Harry Boer argues that the missionary command is its spiritual counterpart in the new creation. "Go therefore and make disciples of all nations . . . You shall be my witnesses . . . to the end of the earth." This, too, is more than an external command. Because of Pentecost it is an organic law of the church's life. We cannot but. Mission was certainly an organic law of the Lord's life on earth. To participate in Christ, as we must do in the

4. Harry Boer, *Pentecost and Missions*.

Eucharist, is to participate in his mission, as we must do in the world.

Every communion service is also a pointer to the messianic banquet when the kingdom is complete. "And men will come from east and west, and from north and south, and sit at table in the kingdom of God" (Lk 13:29, RSV). But how shall they come without an invitation? And how shall they hear without a preacher? And how can men preach unless they are sent? And who will send but the people of God? And who will go but the people of God? No awakened worshiper at our Lord's table today can be unconcerned about the final ingathering—not if he is made to realize that a thousand million people alive now have never heard the name of Jesus. What has happened to the church's proclamation? Do those who are so much enjoying their parish communions enjoy knowing this? We are teaching our people to take an ever greater and more active part in the worship, with our central altars and westward position and offertory processions and the rest. Is all this enclosing them in the church or thrusting them out into mission, making them take a greater and more active part in proclamation? Is the parish communion deepening the sense of commitment to mission? When is every parish in England, or at least every rural deanery, going to think in terms of producing and sending at least one missionary somewhere in every generation? There is not a bishop in any Anglican diocese in Africa, Asia, or the Caribbean who is not asking for missionaries. Yesterday's proclamation of the Gospel by our fathers will not do for today. Each generation must hear it proclaimed afresh by the contemporary people of God—if they are present in the right places and their presence is made effective by prayer.

4. Finally, mission is transformation. This is turning round a phrase of Paul Tillich's, "Transformation is the

meaning of missions." He is referring to what he calls "the attempt to transform the latent church—which is present in the world religions, in paganism, Judaism, and humanism— into something new: the New Reality in Jesus as the Christ."[5] Once again we are faced with a concept which is relevant to worship and to mission alike and is the ultimate goal of both. For the end of all our worship is that we should be transformed into Christ's likeness and that he should be formed in us. And the end of the Christian mission is that the kingdoms of this world become the kingdom of our God and of his Christ. Transformation is part of the sacramental principle and of the missionary principle. In the Eucharist what begins as bread and wine does not remain mere bread and wine. By virtue of human prayer and divine promise something happens. Bread and wine become vehicles for Christ. There is always the process of becoming. Sinners become saints; mere men become prophets and priests, pastors and evangelists; the desert becomes a garden; water becomes wine; Simon becomes Peter, and Saul, St. Paul; those who were no people become the people of God. So it goes on as the hands of God touch history through Christian lives, till shame becomes glory and struggle becomes peace. The mission of the people of God is to be so completely his, that they are agents of this transformation. Pierre Teilhard de Chardin has written about "the divinization of our activities."[6] He says, "the Christian knows that his function is to divinize the world in Jesus Christ."[7] And in an earlier passage he had written: "Any increase that I can bring upon myself or upon things is translated into some increase in my power to love and some progress in Christ's blessed hold

5. "Missions and World History," in *The Theology of the Christian Mission*, p. 284.

6. *The Divine Milieu* (New York: Harpers, 1963), pp. 17-43.

7. *Ibid.*, p. 42.

upon the universe." Behind all this there is profound mystery. As in the Eucharist so in the mission. Before him we can only bow—adoringly in worship, obediently in mission. Through both comes transformation.

Presence, prayer, proclamation, transformation: these are the ways of worship and of mission for the people of God. At the heart of it all is a cross on which something was done "for the sins of the whole world." Of this deed everybody should know. Until they do, the church's task remains unfinished. But until the worshipers at our parish communions know that what they are doing in every Eucharist commits them soul and body to mission, the liturgical movement will not have done its work. Our parishes may need missions. They must become missions.

The Worship of the Church
and the Modern Man

EDGAR S. BROWN, JR.

INTRODUCTION

At the outset we must begin with certain definitions. To use the term "worship" is to focus immediately upon all that the church does within the sphere of its cultic activity. Popular usage has all but divorced this term from its more accurate designation as that total response to God of the grateful Christian. Yet the New Testament evidence is unmistakably clear. St. Paul's admonition to the Roman Christians (12:1) "that ye present your bodies a living sacrifice, holy, acceptable unto God, which is your reasonable service," is far more than a call to cultic performance.

This distinction is important because it demonstrates that the Christian's life cannot be compartmentalized. Whatever he does, be it the celebration of the liturgy or the loving service of his fellow men, all this, so long as it is done "to God," is properly labelled as worship. This is not to infer that man is thereby given a choice between two roads down which he may travel as he responds to God's grace. *Leiturgia* (or cultus) and *Diakonia* (or ethics) are not mutually exclusive. It is not a case of "either-or," but of "both-and." We shall say more of this later.

Having said this, that the force of the term "worship" is so broad as to be designative of all that man does in his response to God, we must now acknowledge that for the purpose of this essay we are here concerned with worship primarily as a cultic phenomenon.

Secondly, we must determine what we mean by "modern man." Since we are dealing with the church in its cultic manifestations, have we to do here only with the Christian "modern man," that specimen, now becoming so rapidly extinct in some areas of Christendom, who by his attendance at services participates, whether knowingly or unknowingly, in the cultic action? If this is what we mean by "modern man," then our course is fixed: to make of the liturgical action a vital, relevant, significant thing to one already committed. This is a task which is challenging, although not impossible.

But is this the end of our responsibility? What of the pagan "modern man" for whom the church has little if any meaning? Since his only contact, if any there be, with the church, is more likely than not with the public services of worship, is there not also a commensurate responsibility to so conduct our cultus that it will have relevance, even appeal, as he struggles to meet the problem of life?

It would seem, therefore, that when we speak of "modern man" we are faced with Tweedledum and Tweedledee, a set of twins in so many ways singularly alike, and in another diametrically opposite. Yet even the problem of making our worship significant to both the Christian "modern man" and the pagan "modern man" is not insurmountable, providing, of course, that we can distinguish our dealings with both, the one from the other. Even so, the distinction is an artificial one. The "modern man" with whom we have to deal is not so neatly pigeon-holed into the precisely defined categories determined above. All too often the church finds itself facing a *tertium quid*—"modern man" in what might be called an intermediate state who, though baptized and maintaining a nominal relationship with the church by making an infrequent appearance at services (festival celebrations, weddings, funerals, etc.), feels little if any compunction to identify with the church's cultus the larger areas of life.

This type of "modern man" and his attitude to the church and its worship is described by Ignaz Silone:

> One fine Sunday some of us stopped going to Mass, not because Catholic dogma seemed to us, all of a sudden, false, but because the people who went began to bore us and we were drawn to the company of those who stayed away . . . what characterized our revolt was the choice of comrades. . . . Without the slightest attempt at resistance, indeed with the well-known fervor of neophytes, one accepts the language, symbols, organization, discipline, tactics, program and doctrine of the party to which one's new comrades belong. It is hardly surprising that rarely should anything learned in the catechism and schoolbooks hinder one's docile acceptance of the new orthodoxy. Indeed, one does not even feel the need of refuting them, because all of that has become part of the world one has left behind. They are neither true nor false; they are "bourgeois," dead leaves. . . .[1]

Obviously, this description fits the man who has gone all the way, but what of the thousands who are neither hot nor cold? What of the drifters, the people for whom religious observances are not much more than quaint customs and folklore, practices, by the way, which are fast being displaced by customs rooted and grounded in completely secular culture? Ought we not be concerned for them also?

It would seem, then, that if we are to talk of the relationship of worship to the "modern man" we must be careful to guard against defining too narrowly what we mean by "modern man." Rather ought we to consider worship as it relates to *modern men,* that is, all mankind, who because

1. Silone, *This is my Philosophy* (Ruskin House), p. 240. Quoted in "The Plea of A Parish Pastor," an essay by Henry E. Horn, *The Living Liturgy,* papers presented at a Conference on Worship by the Department of Worship, ULCA, Nov. 29-30, 1960.

of many and varied stimuli stand in differing relationships to the Gospel.

In the light of the foregoing definitions we find that our basic inquiry in what follows must be directed to the following questions: What are the problems facing the church as it attempts to relate its cultus to the modern man, in whatever his relation to the Gospel, and what can the church do to overcome these problems? Even before the mind has opportunity to catalogue some of these problems, as well as to dwell upon attempted solutions now being experimented with in certain quarters of Christendom, another question insinuates itself into our thinking: do we change the liturgy to suit modern man, or is it the church's task to fit modern man to liturgy?

Some will argue that this is the wrong way to begin. Not only should we *not* even attempt to answer these questions, but the very fact that the questions have been allowed to be asked betrays a lack of understanding on the part of the person raising such questions. Says one Old Testament scholar:

> What is the nature of the act of worship? It is now taken for granted that the purpose of the church is the worship of God, and the starting point for most discussions is that which is done in church on Sunday morning. This is good linguistic method, but poor theology, for the startling fact is that on that basis of biblical usage there is very little authority for calling a church ritual worship of God.[2]

Whether this view can be defended or not is an issue which will have to be considered elsewhere. Nor do I feel that the limits of this article allow for opening up the whole question of the nature of worship itself. Were we to allow this here we

2. George E. Mendehall, "Biblical Faith and Cultic Evolution," *The Lutheran Quarterly,* Vol. V, No. 3 (August, 1953), p. 238.

should have to rehearse the arguments of those who so minimize the cultic action of the church as to make it unnecessary to the church's existence in the world. (One can't help wondering, however, what these "anti-cultists" would put in its place. Is the Christian response only an act of intellectual and/or ethical discipline?) Rather I feel that we must begin where we are. We are here concerned with the cultic action itself, and for that reason I propose to concentrate primarily upon the liturgy.

THE HUMAN PARTY TO THE DIALOGUE OF WORSHIP

The structure of the church's worship patterns. The word "liturgy," like the word "worship," has undergone a metamorphosis. Once used to designate the broader arena of the Christian's response, it came in time to be identified with any cultic pattern of worship. More accurately it signifies one particular rite, the classic combination of the *missa catechumenorum* and the *missa fidelium*. This is the central cultic act of Christian worship which in its unity provides for both the preaching of the sermon and the reception of holy communion. It is in this sense that I plan to use the word "liturgy" in what follows.

If we begin with the liturgy, and by association include also the offices (matins, vespers, the litany, etc.) in our consideration of cultic patterns now in use in the church, we must ask another question: for whose use were and are these forms intended? Obviously the answer is clear, these orders of worship are to be employed by the initiated member of the *corpus Christi*. This is particularly true of the liturgy, as recall, for example, the traditional dismissal of the catechumens which preceded the "unveiling" of the "sacred mysteries."

Does this mean that the preaching of the word, which is so much a part of worship in Protestant churches, has no relevance for the person who is not a member of the *koin-onia*? Krister Stendahl reminds us that Acts 2:42

> ... speaks about teaching rather than preaching. What we have come to call the *kerygma*, the announcement of the Gospel as a creative power to salvation, is in the New Testament directed to the outside world. It is missionary preaching. Within the church this kerygma is referred to as the glorious word by which salvation *was* offered to and accepted by the members of the church. They are now admonished to live accordingly. Even the great christological truths are not promulgated as a creative kerygma to the church; the church is reminded of the grace of God which *came* to them by the Gospel and they are urged to draw the consequences thereof in their daily life. Hence the word is the basis, the Magna Charta, the deed of adoption by which the Christian is what he is and is urged to become what he *really* is in Christ (Rom 6). This is the role of the word in the liturgy. It presupposes a clear distinction between the "at home" of the church and its missionary activity where the two-edged sword of the preaching was handled and its judging and saving power manifested itself.[3]

Considering the kinds of sermons one hears from so many pulpits, one wonders if the preachers have learned to keep this distinction clearly in mind. Moreover, where this distinction is not made in the preaching, what kind of an effect does it have upon the hearers? The same question arises out of any consideration of certain portions of the liturgical rite. What can the recitation of the Creed or the singing of the *Gloria in Excelsis* mean for the non-initiate? And how can an act of confessing one's sins reach the heart of a person for whom the word "sin" is not so much an offense against God as, for example, a petty infraction of some now-out-moded moral code enforced in childhood by a puritanical parent? If we are able to determine nothing else from a

3. Krister Stendahl, "Theology and Liturgy," *The Living Liturgy,* op. cit., p. 13.

scrutiny of our present liturgical forms, we are forced to conclude that they have little if any real significance for any but the faithful, practicing Christian.

The distinction between the Christian modern man and the pagan or agnostic man.   If the church were concerned to make its cultus relevant only to the faithful Christian who was diligent in his devotional obedience, the problem would be singularly clear and the solution relatively easy. A program of education couched in the thought forms and vocabulary familiar to the already initiated member of the family, and applied with vigor to young and old alike, would solve the problem nicely. But, as we said earlier, the church is concerned not only with the "ins" but with the "outs" and with that great segment of the populace that knows not whether it is "in" or "out."

To determine who or what is responsible for this situation ought not detain us now, although honesty demands that we acknowledge that the burden of the responsibility rests upon the church itself. All too often in the past the church has flung wide its doors in a great crusade of missionary zeal, which regrettably has been characterized more by emotional enthusiasm than by any clearly defined strategy of what to do with the people when they do come in. Advertising campaigns urging people to "Come to Church Next Sunday" or "Get a Lift at Church" employ the techniques of the world of commerce and they do reap fruit. But the deeper results, sad to say, are plainly evident. It makes about as much sense to invite an outsider to attend the secret meeting of a Masonic assembly (even if he were allowed to enter) as it does to urge a person who had little understanding of the Gospel to participate in the liturgical action of the Christian fellowship. The visitor to the Masonic lodge wouldn't expect to understand what was happening. "After all," he reasons, "these people are 'peculiar,' and I cannot know what they're doing until I join them and submit to their discipline." Yet seldom if ever is the same logic applied to the church. How often does one hear that the church is a "peculiar" fellowship? Because what is done in the churches is not always immediately meaningful to the occasional visitor, it is the church, not the visitor, who is criticized.

We may take some comfort when we apply this situation to the modern pagan. We ought be less sanguine, however, when we consider that "modern man" who, though reared in the church and frequenting its services from time to time, is in reality indifferent to all that the church stands for. He is a member of the family, albeit an inactive one, and because he is indifferent in performance of his liturgy, the church needs to inquire why he has reached this state. Here perhaps is the most complicated segment of our problem, and the one which we do well to keep uppermost in all that follows. Have we been guilty of assuming that because a man is baptized, been exposed to the customary pre-Confirmation instruction, and then been admitted to the Eucharist, that his life in the Spirit will be derived by a sort of religious osmosis? Has the church kept abreast of man's intellectual explorations, spurred as it has been by scientific, economic and political developments, so as to relate the Gospel with a brilliant relevance to the world in which man lives? These and many more are the sort of questions that ought to concern us as we proceed.

Lest we be diverted from the main stream of our investigation, however, let it be clearly understood that what follows has to do primarily with the meaning and practice of worship as this is employed by the Christian initiate. Only by indirection can we relate our problem to the "outsider." The church must make a clear distinction between evangelism and the "family conversation" of its liturgy.

CRITICISMS LEVELLED AGAINST THE CHURCH'S WORSHIP
FROM WITHIN

Communication.

1. *Language.*   One of the frequently heard criticisms
of Christian worship is directed against its language. Among
Protestants in the United States, the King James Version of
the Bible (1611) continues to lead the field, this in spite of
the best efforts of publishers, advertising techniques, and
parish education specialists to substitute the Revised Standard Version (1952). Most of the Lutherans in America
have a new liturgy which perpetuates the familiar Eliza-
bethan English, but congregations have the option of reading the appointed liturgical lessons from either the KJV or
the RSV. Imagine the result. Shall we read, as we do in the
epistle for Cantate Sunday, "Wherefore lay apart all filthiness and superfluity of naughtiness" (KJV, Jas 1:21), or
shall we instead read, "Therefore put away all filthiness and
rank growth of wickedness" (RSV)? Perhaps we ought to
use the New English Bible: "Away then with all that is
sordid, and the malice that hurries to excess . . ."; or shall
we go a step further and read the translation of J. B. Phillips:
"Have done, then, with impurity and every other evil . . ."
The decisions may be easily made by a comparison of texts.
After all, the language of the liturgy ought to be relevant so
that we do not repeat the error of Rome with its bilingual
missals or of the Russian Church with its archaic Church
Slavonic. But how far does one go? Even the most ardent
devotee of relevance in liturgical speech has difficulty phras-
ing a prayer which uses the modern forms for the second
person of the personal pronoun rather than the more familiar
"thee" and "thou."

There is a deeper issue involved here. Certain words may
be archaic. For them modern substitutes can be found. But

what about those words which while still a part of the contemporary idiom have become so encrusted with "churchliness" that they have little significance in common speech. If the church knows what it means by, for example, the word "redemption," but society identifies this with coupons or "trading stamps," what good is the word to the church's parlance? Henry E. Horn tells of a certain college where freshmen are assigned readings from a pamphlet entitled *Evolution and Religion,* this to introduce them to the prevailing thoughts of modern man. Specifically listed are:

1. Space—Copernicus, *On the Revolution of the Heavenly Bodies,* 1543
2. Time—Lyell, *The Principles of Geology,* 1830-32
3. Life—Darwin, *The Origin of the Species,* 1859
4. Society—Marx, *Das Kapital,* 1867
5. Mind—Freud, *The Interpretation of Dreams,* 1900
6. Method—Einstein, *The Special Theory of Relativity,* 1905

Pastor Horn then continues:

If one can believe that these men actually changed the thought patterns in their various fields of endeavor, then the largest part of man's experience has changed—and all this happened *since the Reformation.* And this in a time when familiarity with the biblical language and typology was fading away. Today the most earnest seekers are again and again blocked and offended by the language of our worship. This offense is muddied by the fundamentalistic memory that most Americans have of the teachings of the church. Though biblical studies and existential psychologies deepen the meanings of the old words in the church, these same words convey strange emotional pictures to the unenlightened, which bring up visions of a narrow literalism of long ago.[4]

Remembering that the church is a "peculiar" society with a "peculiar" conversation, yet which is constituted of persons who also live in the world, are we not in danger of pre-

4. Henry E. Horn, op. cit., p. 7.

senting our people with a choice of being either a schizoid or an ostrich? The cross may be foolishness or a stumbling block to those who will not or cannot accept it, but must it be clothed in unintelligible speech and ideas?

2. *Tradition.*   Along with the wealth of its insistence upon an active apostolate in both cultus and life, the liturgical movement has opened the door to a repristination of the rites, ceremonies and furnishings for worship from other ages of the church's history. In those segments of Protestantism which have experienced the ravages of rationalism and pietism, this development has had a wholesome effect upon worship. In place of lengthy services filled with verbose prayers and exhortations, ponderous sermons, and little music save the singing of pietistic hymns, we now enjoy rites which restore to the people their rightful liturgy. The ordinary of the Mass, derived mainly from the classic Western rite and Luther's liturgical revisions together with the better church orders of the sixteenth century, forms the basis of customary Lutheran Sunday worship. Church buildings employ the best of the artist's crafts; clergy and choirs are now vested in traditional garb, and ceremonial practices have added a dimension to the cultus.

Yet all this has not been without criticism. Some have properly cautioned against a rigid liturgical order which allows no room for development.

> . . . What at one time was decisive in the history of the liturgy is not an indisputable necessity for the presentday congregation. The liturgical creativity of the spirit in the contemporary congregation dare not be disregarded. It is, therefore, always dangerous to enforce forms upon a congregation which were produced in another era. A liturgical revival dare not take as its ultimate goal the mere renaissance of discarded liturgical forms.[5]

5. Vilmos Vajta, "The Theological Basis and Nature of Liturgy," *The Lutheran World,* Vol. VI, No. 3 (December, 1959), p. 239 f.

Vajta's point is well taken, but I take it to mean that he is not saying that some repristination, if it serves the upbuilding of the congregation, is not invalid. To listen to some modern "iconoclasts" is to draw another inference. Any effort to improve worship, if it draws from the past, is, according to these critics, nothing more than "antiquarianism" or "estheticism." To cite but a few examples of the criticism levelled among American Lutherans:

(1) the use of the surplice by American Lutheran clergymen is improper because it is an "Anglican importation,"

(2) sanctuary lamps ". . . are to be avoided because of their association with the doctrine of transubstantiation," and

(3) the celebration of the Holy Communion in educational institutions is to be "discouraged" because this is "primarily the responsibility of the organized congregation."

Relevance.   No one will dispute the fact that the church has a paramount responsibility to make its cultic action intelligible to its people. This should be true in every area of communication, be it the spoken or sung word, the actions of the participants, or the accoutrements and the place of worship itself. In this last we would place vestments, furnishings, symbols, art forms, and the like. Whether it be a painted Chi-Rho on the soffit of an arch, the colored stole, or the spoken word, all these ought to "speak" intelligibly to the initiated beholder.

But the church is not an *ad hoc* assembly, created especially for this gathering of the people at a particular time in a particular place. It enjoys a history, and so has a heritage. The marks of this heritage are a part of its life. Because at one time the church spoke Greek, the liturgy still prefers to label its opening litany the *Kyrie*. Latin terms still survive as brief, yet adequate, titles for many portions of liturgical expressions, not to mention theological explication. Vestments in use today are not greatly unlike those worn fifteen hundred years ago, and the same can be said for ceremonies, rites and furnishings.

To many of the critics of current cultic practice in the church, the so-called liturgical revival is little more than unabashed romanticism. Completely impervious to the urgent demands of an anxiety-infected society, the modern devotees of the Christian cultus, say their critics, are "playing church" while Rome burns. It is a lot easier, and much more pleasant, to debate the color and shape of chasubles than to be afire for social justice or political freedom, not to mention the infinitely greater concerns for faith and grace. Unfortunately, there is just enough truth in some of this criticism to make it valid. Says Ernest B. Koenker in his *Worship in Word and Sacrament:*

> Do the Gregorian chant, vestments, and candles actually contribute to the spiritual edification of the worshiper, or are they merely an aesthetic consideration? Liturgy may become something vaguely sentimental or a cult of the beautiful. Instead of worshiping God in the "beauty of holiness" we worship him in the "holiness of beauty." Beauty then exercises a demonic spell over the worshiper that blocks any real encounter with God. Liturgical forms no longer act as bearers of the holy but are viewed as holy in themselves. So the possibility of entering a relationship with the holy, the source of man's life and righteousness, is prevented by an idolatrous attachment to symbols robbed of their transparency.[6]

Certainly no churchman would wish to so pervert the liturgy as to vitiate its effectiveness as a vehicle of the Gospel, but does the fault rest solely with the forms that the cultic action takes? Is the quest for relevance, so ardently espoused by the anti-liturgical "crepe-hangers," simply to be resolved by providing new cultic patterns in a language and an action

6. E. B. Koenker, *Worship in Word and Sacrament* (St. Louis: Concordia Publishing House, 1959), p. 73.

that is easily understandable to all comers? If it is true, as the critics say, that the liturgy fails to have significant relevance to the "modern man," then is man's attitude conditioned by the forms of worship or by what those forms intend to convey? It would seem to me that the answers to these questions lie in the fact that no liturgical form will make sense to its user, be he an active or passive participant, unless he is knowledgeable of the meanings of the symbols used therein.

Congregational Passivity and the weakening of the Christian Response.

1. *In the cult.*   It is most unfortunate that in those churches which did so much in the Reformation to restore the role of the people to genuinely corporate worship, there is so little appreciation of the fact that the liturgy is "the people's work." Instead of recognizing that he, along with his fellow Christians, has a responsibility to fulfill our Lord's command to "do this in remembrance of me," modern man instead looks upon worship as an activity of professionals. Thus he becomes a spectator at a "performance" presided over by clergy, choirs, acolytes and ushers, and because he looks upon himself as a spectator he soon feels that he has the right (some even look upon it as a responsibility) to judge the "performance" in much the same way as he criticizes a play or concert.

What is the reason for this attitude? Undoubtedly some of the liturgies in use in the churches at different times have contributed to what we call "spectatoritis." If the people were given little or nothing to do, while the minister appeared to do everything, then it was inevitable that this situation would develop. I wonder, however, if the reason does not lie far deeper. Can it be that the interpretation so often heard in Lutheran articles (which stresses so persistently the role of God in worship, almost to the exclusion of man's part in the dialogue), has encouraged congregational passivity in Lutheran churches? Does the Lutheran insistence upon the gift in worship tend to give the cultus, and particularly the liturgy, such an *it-centeredness* that man feels he need do nothing? If we criticize the pre-Reformation church for that liturgical corruption which made of the priest an intermediary whose duty it was to say Mass *for* the people, have we not simply shifted the problem by requiring that the minister provide Holy Communion *for* the people? If the burden of our theology stresses so strongly the notion that the liturgy is God's gift to us, without providing commensurate opportunity for the place to be given to our response to that gift, then the rite is celebrated for no other reason than the distribution of the gift. I go to church, therefore, in order to get, not to carry on a dialogue. Says J. A. T. Robinson in his book *Liturgy Coming to Life:*

> The parson becomes a sort of garage proprietor whose job is to be open (weekly, monthly, daily, according to demand) for any of his customers who require to fill up. Who comes and how often depends, quite naturally, on what the individual thinks he needs and how much he feels he gets from it.[7]

But where then is the liturgy of not only the minister, but of all the faithful? If the word, by its very nature, demands that man respond either in faith or in unbelief, what then, in what we tend to call worship, is man's response? And, how does man make his response if, as so often happens in our churches, he is nothing more than a spectator? The very word "liturgy" is a lie unless all of the members of the body take an active part in the divine-human dialogue.

If this attitude of the modern churchman, as outlined above, characterizes the worship that is celebrated at the

---

7. J. A. T. Robinson, *Liturgy Coming to Life* (London: A. R. Mowbray & Co., Ltd., 1960), p. 60.

time of the assembling of the congregation (and what other occasion for assembling the entire congregation is observed with greater or even equal frequency?), what shall be the result of man's devotional life in smaller assemblies (parish societies, auxiliaries, etc.) and in his individual prayer life? And how can he move from a passivity in the cultus to a genuinely Christian activity in society?

2. *In group and private devotional life.* The subdivisions of the congregation have specific purposes and causes, yet all are alike in that each draws its spiritual sustenance from worship. Thus the patterns of group worship on this level are but an extension of the worship of the total congregation. Whether the forms of the officially accepted patterns decreed by the church (e.g., matins, vespers, the litany, etc.) or specially prepared patterns including psalms, lessons, prayers and hymns, they should provide for group participation, be revelant to the exigencies of life, and communicate clearly. Unfortunately, much of what passes for "devotions" in the meetings of parish groups is little more than a bow in the direction of propriety, something to be done before turning to "more important matters." Such an attitude betrays a lack of understanding of the meaning of the cultus. It encourages a notion held by many a churchgoer who usually regards the liturgical rite as nothing more than a frame for the sermon. This attitude also fails to reckon with the existence of the *ecclesiola* and the *Ecclesia*. Though the gathering be but a few in numbers it is still the place where God and man meet to share in the dialogue intended to affect all of man's existence. And it is only as this dialogue is carried on with intelligence and enthusiasm that all that follows can really make sense.

What has been said for group devotions must be repeated and amplified for private devotions. In spite of the tendency to engage in such exercises in a perfunctory manner, it must be borne firmly in mind that no man prays or meditates as an individual. Always, although he performs his devotions "in his closet," he is part of the church at worship.

3. *In society.* The American Roman Catholic priest, H. A. Reinhold, says: "We all know of daily communicants who fail to be a witness in their circles and whose only mark of lived religion seems to be their daily Holy Communion and what it involves." Deploring this sort of monad Christianity, Reinhold says that "it is like high-octane gas in a broken-down, one cylinder motor."[8]

Here we come face to face with the most alarming condemnation of the church's cultic activity. What if after all our scholarly and poetic effort to provide cultic patterns that are both beautiful and relevant, our determined programs to train the people in their "proper" conduct of the liturgy, our enthusiastic sponsorship of the best in music and art . . . what if after having done all these, our cultus has failed to influence life? The following indictment of Jewish worship by Abraham Heschel applies with equal force to what can happen in the Christian Church:

> Services are conducted with dignity and precision. The rendition of the liturgy is smooth. Everything is present: decorum, voice, ceremony. But one thing is missing: Life. One knows in advance what will ensue. There will be no surprise, no adventure of the soul: There will be no sudden outburst of devotion. Nothing is going to happen to the soul. Nothing unpredictable must happen to the person who prays. He will attain no new perspective for the life he lives. Our motto is monotony. The first has gone out of our worship. It is cold, stiff, dead. True, things are happening: of course, not within prayer, but within the administration of the temple.[9]

8. H. A. Reinhold, *The Dynamics of Liturgy* (New York: Macmillan, 1960), p. 16.

9. Abraham Heschel, *Man's Search for God*, p. 49. Quoted in Henry E. Horn, op. cit., p. 8.

I say this could also be an indictment of Christian worship, and it rises to accuse the Christian Church if what we do in the cultus does not expand into life.

Yet look at the liturgy. The first post-communion collect of the liturgy in the American Lutheran *Service Book and Hymnal* leaves no doubt about the purpose of our eucharistic celebration:

> We give thanks to Thee, Almighty God, that thou hast refreshed us with this thy salutary gift; and we beseech thee, of thy mercy to strengthen us through the same gift, *in faith toward thee and in fervent love toward one another*. . . .

The dimension of the eucharistic response is both vertical and horizontal. Says J. A. T. Robinson, "The sharing of Bread, concluded now sacramentally, must be continued socially—and thence economically and politically,"[10] and again, "The Communion is social dynamite, if we really take seriously the pattern of community known at the altar."[11] Any cultic pattern of worship, whether in the congregation or by an individual, is a mummery unless the conversation and action begun before the altar is continued in every moment of man's existence.

Says the aged archbishop in Bruce Marshal's *Satan and Cardinal Campbell:* "Two things can save the world: prayer and thought. But the trouble is that the people who think, don't pray, and the people who pray, don't think." Just as all of the deep-seated cogitations of theological inquiry are little more than a playing with words and images unless they find their fruition in the active obedience to the Gospel in our dealings with men and with God, so the divorce between liturgy and life betrays an attitude which, if not checked, will make of the church little more than a harmless yet pathetic society of antique-lovers. Liturgy without ethics is sterile.

10. Robinson, op. cit., p. 26.
11. *Ibid.*, p. 37.

Ethics without liturgy is pagan. Well indeed ought we consider the proposal of Gustaf Aulen who says that Gustaf Wingren,

> suggests that the connection of the Holy Communion with mutual, human fellowship would have found a more prominent place "had not the deterioration of the idea of sacrifice through the sacrifice of the mass made Luther so excessively suspicious of any mention of sacrifice." The combination of liturgical and social elements which is found in Anglican piety "must be accepted as a Christian heritage which we Lutherans unfortunately have lost."[12]

THE DIRECTION OF RECOVERY

It would be absurd to suggest that the current difficulties facing the church which have been cited above could be resolved simply by fashioning new and different liturgical rites. The most extreme departure from the traditional forms now in use in the churches (and this has been done, as witness the several attempts to set the classic Mass to jazz, and the translation of the ancient texts to the *koine* of the beatnik) holds little hope for intelligible and obedient participation in the cultus without a basic understanding of that which lies behind our cultic symbols.

How then shall we proceed? Luther's admonition to the clergy of Luebeck in 1530 is as appropriate for us today as it was then:

> . . . do not begin with innovations in rites. . . . Put first and foremost what is fundamental in our teaching, the doctrine concerning justification, namely, that we are justified by another's righteousness, even Christ's, which is given to us in faith and which by God's grace is apprehended by those who are first terrified by the law and who, struck by the consciousness of their sins, sigh for redemption. . . . Reform of impious rites

---

12. Gustaf Aulen, translated by E. H. Wahlstrom, *Eucharist and Sacrifice* (Philadelphia: Muhlenberg Press, 1958), p. 80.

will come of itself when what is fundamental in our teaching, being effectively presented, has taken root in pious hearts.[13]

No cultic pattern, no matter how clear its theological expression, is ever adequate to corporate worship, unless it be intended (which God forbid!) that the regular assemblies of the congregation are nothing more than instructional in purpose. Nor should it be expected that the beauty of poetic imagery and expression in the liturgy can engender a devotion which is not rooted in understanding. Education, therefore, is the primary requisite. But where does one commence the process?

It is patently absurd to expect people to participate in worship forms so reliant upon the biblical idiom if those same people have next to no knowledge of the Scriptures. How can the majestic strains of the opening lines of the *Gloria in Excelsis,* for example, convey the force of the incarnation except there be knowledge of the Bethlehem-event? How does one understand the *Benedictus qui venit* who knows not Palm Sunday, or the *Agnus Dei* without Good Friday? It is impossible for the church to couch its cultic language without drawing upon the Scriptures, and this, of course, implies that the people must know the Bible.

A necessary concomitant of Bible study is training in theology. It is one thing to familiarize people with the contents of the Bible; it is another to get them to so adapt the fruit of that study that they see clearly before them the path of their Christian obedience. I need not stress the point; its import is clear. Rather let me express a concern for what I have come to feel is all too often a failing in too many quarters. Theological investigations are necessary. They are not, however, an end in themselves. In spite of the fascination

13. WA, Br, V, 220, 221. Translated in "Letters of Spiritual Counsel," edited by T. G. Tappert, *The Library of Christian Classics,* Vol. XVIII (Philadelphia: Westminster Press, 1955), p. 296 f.

most of us share in the pursuit of knowledge, which we trust will unfold to our gaze more and more about the nature and work of God, we need to remember that gnosticism, under whatever outward trappings, is still a heresy. The Athanasian Creed should be our beacon: "And the Catholic faith is this: that *we worship (veneremur) one God in Trinity, and Trinity in Unity.*"

What Gordon W. Ireson has to say about the Church of England is true throughout Christendom: "For the vast majority of people in this country *worship must be preceded by instruction, and instruction must be followed by training in worship.*"[14] But this instruction is more than training in liturgical technique, although that is a part, albeit a minor one, of it. Rather we have to do with what Louis Bouyer calls the liturgical principle, "and this liturgical principle is, that we must not try to provide an artificial congregation to take part in an antiquarian liturgy, but rather to prepare the actual congregation of the church today to take part in the truly traditional rightly understood."[15]

Some will argue that this is unnecessary. After all, doesn't the sermon achieve this purpose? Why should the church, faced as it is with so desperate a situation, take time from its heavily-crowded schedule to teach people how to understand and perform cultic rite? But, we must ask also, what is the effect of this cultic set upon our people?

A. G. Hebert says:

> By the influence of the church service the regular church people are moulded; for the things which they do in church make a deeper impression than the teaching which reaches their minds. Often they have thought that they came to church chiefly to hear the sermon. This, however, they forgot; but there were

14. Gordon W. Ireson, *Church Worship and the Non-Churchgoer* (London: SPCK, 1945), p. 22.

15. Louis Bouyer, *Liturgical Piety* (Notre Dame, Indiana: Notre Dame Press, 1954), p. 15.

responses and prayers, commandments, creeds and scriptures, which impressed themselves on their mind by constant repetition. All these things, the church building and the ritual and the ceremonies which take place in it, speak of the reality of God after a manner different in kind from the exhortations of the preacher.[16]

Liturgy is both impression and expression, the vehicle for a dialogue between man and God which may and can go both ways at the same time. With the lips, the worshiper may sing but words, but if he has been enlightened by *training in worship* he is also receiving a deeper appreciation of the words and the actions he has been taught to use. One could make an extended exercise in devotion, for example, by dwelling upon but one short phrase of the *Gloria in Excelsis:* "Thou only art Holy." Or take the *verba Domini* of the Eucharist. These familiar words, seen both in their historical situation and as a parallel to what the contemporary Christian does as a part of his liturgy, unfold the Christian obedience both as to cultus and to life:

Our Lord . . . *took* bread and . . . wine . . .

This is the offertory which provides for the offering of our gifts as a symbol of ourselves. As we set apart the bread and the wine in the cultus, so we offer our lives in service to our fellow men.

. . . And when he had *given thanks* . . .

Here is the great *anamnesis* which, with its recollection of the night of betrayal, makes contemporary the events of Calvary and the first Easter.

. . . He *gave* . . . to his disciples

By the action of eating and drinking all who share in the family meal are strengthened to their continuing apostolate of obedience.

16. A. G. Hebert, *Liturgy and Society* (Naperville, Ill.: Allenson, 1960), p. 39.

It will be seen that through instruction in the meaning of worship, encouragement to participate will come of itself. Just as a member of the cast of a dramatic production would never think of "cutting" the performance simply because he wants an evening off, so the initiated Christian will see his responsibility to be a part of the family's celebration of the living God in the performance of its liturgy.

Moreover, he will come to recognize the value of symbols and signs. The scene in Bernard Shaw's *St. Joan,* where only after a soldier has fashioned a crude cross from two twigs thus giving the martyr courage to face the flames, is a forceful witness to the use of matter in worship. The ceremonies, the furnishings, the gestures and other accoutrements of the cultus may evoke sneering derision from the more sophisticated, but it must never be forgotten that in just such a use of matter can the faith of "one of these little ones" be strengthened. If the adornment of liturgical activity has been accompanied in recent times in the churches by a revival of pre-Reformation practices, we need to inquire into the cause for this repristination. And before we would discard such adornment and make substitution of that which fails to speak to our people, we do well to pause and determine our motives.

What we have just said points, I hope, to the need for renewed attention to, and activity in, the meaning and practice of worship. We have not as yet determined who shall be the subject of this instruction. Ireson, in his book *Church Worship and the Non-Churchgoer,* suggests that we not invite outsiders to our liturgical worship. For those who are outside the church, he suggests the restoration of the catechumenate. This would be a period of training in worship, beginning with guided silence, instruction, bidding prayers, etc. Only after he has evidenced his understanding of the action of this "peculiar" people should the neophyte be admitted to the Christian assembly. Peter Hammond tells of a structure in India

> where the church is approached through a narthex containing a large tank, which stretches across its entire width. All unbaptized persons must remain to the west of this tank until they pass through doors placed to the east of the narthex, and opening directly into the room for the eucharistic assembly.[17]

Such experiments are evidence of the growing desire to restore to the *whole* people of God the fullness of their liturgical ministry—both inside and outside the church. It is not enough to expect that the layman will simply take a pious yet passive role in either cultus or life. The universal priesthood has far wider implication than cultic practices heretofore have allowed. And it is precisely as he exercises his cultic priesthood to the full that his liturgy is made to be felt in all of life.

CONCLUSION

But all this cannot come about unless things are stirred up in the churches. Fortunately, things are beginning to move. Peter Hammond, whose exciting book, *Liturgy and Architecture,* has done much to encourage the discussions, says:

> It is fast becoming a commonplace to observe that western Christendom is in the throes of a new reformation. Not since the sixteenth century has there been such a calling into question of received traditions or such a ferment of experiment. The sources of Christian tradition are being examined afresh in the light of modern biblical and historical scholarship. Theology has begun to shake off the influence of scholasticism and is rediscovering its biblical, patristic and liturgical roots. There is a new sense of the meaning of the church as the people of God and the body of Christ. A deepened understanding of the Eucharist, and of its social implications, has transformed the

17. Peter Hammond, *Liturgy and Architecture* (London: Barrie & Rockliffe, 1960), p. 46.

life of many a parish and has effected something of a revolution in the celebration of the liturgy itself.[18]

The compelling promulgation of its doctrines and the loving service of its patterns of ethics may restore to the church the greater sphere of influence it desires for the Gospel. Yet always there must be that other activity of Christian obedience which nurtures the believer in his intimate relation with God. Thinking, knowing and teaching, together with unselfish service of one's fellows, can only draw their inspiration at the wellsprings of corporate devotion. In no other area of its activity does the church touch the lives of men with quite the same potential for impulsion to love that it does in its worship. The investigations into the meaning and practice of the cultus, and the accompanying experiments born of imagination, portend a hopeful sign. If these will but bear fruit in parish churches throughout the world— among the family of God—the future looms bright for the Gospel.

18. Ibid., p. 13.

THE CONTRIBUTORS

The Rev. Arthur M. Allchin, an Anglican priest, is Librarian of Pusey House, Oxford, England, and editor of *Sobornost,* a quarterly particularly interested in Anglican-Orthodox inter-faith concerns.

The Rev. Dr. Cyril C. Richardson, an Episcopal priest, is Dean of Graduate Studies, Union Theological Seminary, New York City.

Nicolas Zernov, a Russian Orthodox lay theologian, is Spalding Lecturer in Eastern Orthodox Culture, Oxford, England.

The Rev. Dr. George W. Webber, a minister of the United Church of Christ, is Associate Professor of Church and Community, Union Theological Seminary and also Director of Metropolitan Urban Service Training Facility, New York City.

The Rev. Max Thurian, theologian and liturgist, is sub-prior of the Reformed monastery of Taizé, Seine et Loire, France.

The Rev. Roger Greenacre, an Anglican priest, is Chaplain of Liddon House, London, England.

The Rev. Dr. Harald Riesenfeld, a Lutheran minister of the Church of Sweden, is Professor of Biblical Exegesis, the University of Uppsala, Uppsala, Sweden.

The Rev. Dr. Thomas F. Torrance, a minister of the Church of Scotland, is Professor of Christian Dogmatics, University of Edinburgh, Edinburgh, Scotland, and Editor of the *Scottish Journal of Theology*.

The Rev. Boris Bobrinskoy, archpriest, is Professor of Dogmatic Theology at St. Sergius Institute of Orthodox Theology, Paris, France.

The Rev. Dr. Massey H. Shepherd, Jr., an Episcopal priest, is Professor of Liturgics at the Church Divinity School of the Pacific, Berkeley, California.

The Rev. Douglas Webster, Honorary Canon of Chelmsford, is Professor of Mission at Selly Oak Colleges, Birmingham, England, and Examining Chaplain for the Bishop of Chelmsford.

The Rev. Dr. Edgar S. Brown, Jr., a Lutheran minister, is Director of the Commission on Worship of the Lutheran Church in America, New York City.